Sequel to *Breaking Through* and *The Circuit*

Reaching Out

Francisco Jiménez

Houghton Mifflin Company

Boston 2008

www.houghtonmifflinbooks.com

The text of this book is set in Goudy.

Photos are from the author's private collection.

Library of Congress Cataloging-in-Publication Data is on file.

ISBN-13: 978-0-618-03851-0

Manufactured in the United States of America
MP 10 9 8 7 6 5 4 3 2 1

To my family and the community of my alma mater,
Santa Clara University

Acknowledgments

I would like to thank my mother, Joaquina; my brothers, Roberto, José Francisco, Juan Manuel, and Rubén; my sister, Avelina; my sister-in-law, Darlene; my wife, Laura; and my friends Smokey Murphy and Emily Bernabé for providing me with their own personal recollections of the period I write about in this book. Special thanks to my immediate family—Laura, Francisco "Pancho," Lori, Carlo, Dario, Camille, Miguel, Susanna, Tomás, and Nova—for patiently listening to drafts and offering helpful comments.

I wish to thank the community of my childhood for being a constant inspiration to me in my writing and in my personal and professional life.

I have a lasting gratitude to my teachers, whose guidance and faith in my ability helped me break through many barriers. I thank them for reaching out to me and for responding when I reached out to them for help in my educational journey. They inspired me to reach out to other learners, especially first-generation college students.

Thanks to my colleagues and friends, especially Father Paul Locatelli, S.J. Don Dodson, Alma García, and Susan Erickson, for encouraging me to continue writing.

A special thanks to Ann Rider, my wonderful editor, for her valuable suggestions for improvements and her gentle insistence that I write from the heart.

Contents

College Bound

The day I had longed for had finally arrived. It was Sunday, September 9, 1962. I felt excited and nervous as I got ready to make the trip north to Santa Clara. I had worked hard to make this journey to college even though it seemed improbable for so many years.

I did not anticipate, however, how difficult it would be to leave my family, especially my older brother, Roberto.

Roberto and I had been inseparable ever since we were children living in El Rancho Blanco, a small village nestled on barren, dry hills in the northern part of the state of Jalisco, Mexico. I called him "Toto" because when I was first learning to talk, I could not pronounce "Roberto." In Mexico, he used to take me to church on Sundays. In the evenings, he and I huddled with our parents around a fire built with dry cow chips in the middle of our adobe hut and listened to our uncle Mauricio tell ghost stories. I kept Roberto company every day while he milked our five cows by hand before dawn, and I helped him fetch water from the river. I cried every time Toto was out of my sight. Whenever

I misbehaved, my parents punished me by separating me from him.

Hoping to leave our poverty behind and start a new and better life, my family emigrated illegally from Mexico to California in the late 1940s and began working in the fields. From the time I was six years old, Toto and I worked together alongside our parents. He sang Mexican songs to me such as "Cielito Lindo" and "Dos Arbolitos" while we picked cotton in early fall and winter in Corcoran. After we were deported in 1957 by *la migra* and came back legally, Roberto took care of me like a father when he and I lived alone for six months in Bonetti Ranch, a migrant labor camp. He was a sophomore in high school and I was in the eighth grade at the time. The rest of our family stayed in Guadalajara and joined us later. During that time, I helped him in his job doing janitorial work at Main Street School in Santa Maria after school, and on weekends we worked together topping carrots or thinning lettuce. After graduating from high school, Roberto got married and continued working as a custodian for the Santa Maria School District on weekdays. And even though he had left our home in Bonetti Ranch to start his own family, we saw each other often. On weekends he and I worked together for the Santa Maria Window Cleaners, a commercial janitorial company.

Roberto and his wife, Darlene, dropped by early that Sunday morning with their baby girl, Jackie, to say goodbye. Darlene, who looked a lot like the actress Elizabeth Taylor, patted Roberto on the back, trying to console him, while he and I hugged each other. "He'll be back for Thanksgiving," she said. Being separated from my brother was as painful as yanking out a fingernail.

My father was in one of his usual bad moods and impatient to get going. "*Vámonos, pues,*" he said annoyed. Let's get going.

Ever since he had hurt his back from doing stoop labor for many years and could no longer work in the fields, his temper had gotten worse. Bracing himself on Roberto's broad shoulders, he carefully slid onto the passenger's seat of our old, beat-up DeSoto. His face was pale and drawn and his eyes were red from lack of sleep. He was upset because I was leaving home. He wanted our family to always be together.

I locked the front door to the army barrack, which we rented from Mr. Bonetti. I climbed in the driver's seat, slammed the bent door shut, and quickly fastened it with a rope to keep it closed. As we drove out of Bonetti Ranch, I rolled down the cracked window so I could make hand signals. My father flinched every time the car hit potholes in the dusty road. Trampita, my younger brother, sat between my father and me. We gave José Francisco the nickname "Trampita," Little Tramp, because my parents dressed him in baby clothes we found in the city dump when he was born. My other younger brothers, Torito and Rubén, and my little sister, Rorra, sat in the back seat with my mother. They were excited to make the trip, but they kept quiet because my father did not tolerate noise, especially when he was in a bad mood.

I turned right onto East Main and headed west on the two-lane road toward Santa Maria to take Highway 101 north to Santa Clara. The sun poked its head above the mountains behind us, casting a shadow in front of our DeSoto. On both sides of the narrow road were hundreds of acres of strawberry fields, which my family had worked in during the harvest season, from sunup to sundown, a few years before. As we approached the Santa Maria Bridge, I remembered the pain I felt every time we had crossed this bridge on our way north to Fresno to pick grapes and cotton every September for eight years. During that time I always missed the first ten weeks of school because I was working with my family in the fields.

From the corner of my eye I saw my father close his eyes. "Do you want me to drive, Panchito?" Trampita whispered. "You look tired." My family called me "Panchito," the Spanish nickname for Francisco, which was my birth name.

"No, thanks. You need to rest yourself. You'll have to drive back."

Trampita had to take over my janitorial job and work thirty-five hours a week, as I did, while going to school to help support our family. Without him, I would not have been making this journey.

Through the rearview mirror I saw my mother dozing off with her arms around Rorra and Rubén, who were fidgety.

Torito gazed out the side window, humming something to himself.

We called Rubén, my youngest brother, Carne Seca, because he was as thin as a strip of beef jerky when he was a child. He sat on my father's lap whenever we traveled from place to place, following the crops. My father favored him because, according to my mother, Rubén looked like my dad.

Rorra, my little sister, whose given name was Avelina, followed me around whenever I was home. She liked being teased, and often when we poked fun at each other, she would remind me of the time she was four years old and took two of my favorite pennies from my coin collection and bought gum with them from a gum machine. "I am stuck on you," she'd say, laughing. We called her Rorra, "doll," because she looked like one. We all doted on her.

I felt a pain in my chest, thinking about not seeing them every day.

We passed familiar coastal towns along the way: Nipomo, Arroyo Grande, Pismo Beach. As we approached San Luis Obispo, I remembered visiting California Polytechnic College during my junior year. Now I was headed to the University of Santa Clara, and the only thing I knew about college for sure was that it would be more difficult than high school. I knew this because Mrs. Taylor, my freshman social studies teacher, often told our class, "You think the work I give you is hard? Wait until you go to college!"

Our DeSoto strained to climb the San Luis Obispo grade.

There was a string of cars behind me. "Move to the right and let cars pass you," my father said, waking up from his nap.

"I can see why you didn't get a good grade in driver's ed," Trampita said, laughing. I elbowed Trampita in the shoulder and steered to the right lane. The driver behind me gave me a nasty look as he passed by. I kept my eyes straight ahead, avoiding eye contact with the other drivers.

"I hope I don't get a ticket for driving so slow."

"Like your father," my mother said, tapping my father on the back of the head. My father was not amused. He had been stopped by the highway patrol a couple of times on our way to Fresno for driving our *carcachita,* our old jalopy, too slowly. He was not cited either time because we gave the officer the excuse that our mattress, which was on top of the car roof, would fly off if he drove too fast, even though it was tied with ropes to the front and rear bumpers.

The heat increased as we continued north past Atascadero and Paso Robles.

Rorra said she was hungry.

"*Yo también tengo hambre,*" Rubén agreed.

"We'll stop in King City," my mother said as we passed by the sign for the turnoff.

"No, let's wait until we get to Santa Clara," my father said firmly. "*Aguántense!*" Put up with it. There was dead silence. A half-hour later, Rorra and Rubén made it known again that they were hungry.

"My stomach is making funny noises," Rorra said

sheepishly, rubbing her stomach with her right hand.

"What's it saying?" my father asked, chuckling.

"It wants food."

"Mine too," Rubén chimed in.

"How about stopping in Soledad?" my mother suggested, noticing that my father was in a better mood.

"No, it will bring us bad luck," my father quickly objected. I understood my father's objection—*soledad* means "loneliness" or "a lonely place" in Spanish. I disagreed with him, but I didn't contradict him. I knew better. "As soon as you see an open area, pull over," my father said, lighting up a cigarette.

We approached a long row of tall eucalyptus trees along the left bank of the highway, right outside of King City. I slowed down and made a left turn onto a narrow dirt road and continued for a quarter of a mile, followed by a cloud of dust, and parked the car on the side of the road. "Thanks for bringing us to the desert," Trampita said. "I am sure our *taquitos* will taste better with a little dust on them."

"*Qué chistoso,*" my mother said, laughing. Very funny. My father looked at me and smiled.

"This isn't dust, Trampita. It's powdered salsa."

"*Ya pues,*" my mother said. Enough. "Let's eat." She took an army blanket from the trunk of the car and a large brown grocery bag, which she handed to Torito. She spread the blanket on the ground for us to sit on. Trampita and I helped our dad sit with his back leaning against the front right tire.

"I made these *taquitos* with chorizo and eggs this morning," my mother said proudly as she handed them out. Rubén and Rorra gobbled their tacos and asked for another one.

"*Que los mantenga el gobierno,*" my father said. Only the government can afford to feed them.

"That's for sure," my mother said, lightly stroking Rorra's hair. "You'd better eat a couple more, Panchito. You won't get these at the university."

I had not thought about what the food would be like at college until my mother mentioned it. Beginning in middle school, Roberto asked her not to make us tacos for our school lunch because kids made fun of us. So she made us sandwiches instead but always put a chile pepper with the sandwich to add flavor.

We continued our trip through the Salinas Valley, which looked like a huge, colorful tapestry. It was bordered by mountain ranges to the west and cut in the middle by a black strip of road that stretched as far as the eye could see. Along the way were acres and acres of lettuce, cauliflower, celery, vineyards, and strawberries, and yellow, red, purple, and white flowers. "It looks like paradise, a green heaven," my mother said, in awe.

"Not for people working the fields," my father countered.

I agreed with him. Every few miles I saw a string of old, dusty cars and pickup trucks parked on the edge of the fields, and clusters of farm workers hunched over, picking the crops or hoeing weeds. Our own family had done the same kind of work year after year for the first nine years we were in California.

As we entered Salinas, I remembered that this was John Steinbeck's birthplace. Miss Bell, my sophomore-year English teacher, had asked me to read *The Grapes of Wrath* after she had read an essay I wrote about Trampita. The novel was difficult to read because I was still struggling with the English language, but I could not put it down. I identified with the Joad family. Their experiences were like my own family's, as well as those of other migrant workers. I was moved by their story, and for the first time I had read something in school to which I could relate.

"You're going too fast. Slow down, Panchito!" my father exclaimed, pressing his right foot against the floorboard.

I was so absorbed in my thoughts that I did not notice I was speeding. We passed through Gilroy and Morgan Hill and entered San José. It was large and cosmopolitan compared to Santa Maria, which had only 28,000 people. My heart began to beat faster as I drove north on The Alameda.

"I think we're getting closer," I said. "I believe The Alameda becomes El Camino Real, but I'm not sure."

"What do you mean, you're not sure?" my father asked. "What's the address?"

"I don't know," I said apologetically, confused. "I know it's on El Camino Real in Santa Clara." I pulled into a Texaco gas station and Trampita got out to ask for directions.

My father was upset. He was biting his lower lip and searching in his shirt pocket for a cigarette.

"We're okay," Trampita said as he slid back into the front seat next to my father. "Keep going on The Alameda for another mile until it becomes El Camino Real. El Camino Real goes right through the university."

I sighed in relief. I pulled out of the gas station and continued on The Alameda, which was lined with spruce and sycamore trees and large Spanish colonial–style homes.

"*Mira*, Panchito," my mother said. Look. "Those houses look like the ones in the rich part of Guadalajara. They're beautiful."

I looked in the rearview mirror. My mother seamed sad. She had always wanted a house of our own, but no matter where we lived, whether it was in an old garage, a tent, or an army barrack, she always made it our home. She displayed Mexican knickknacks, like miniature ceramic dogs or birds, and placed cut wildflowers in a vase on whatever crate or box happened to serve as our table. "*Nuestra casa*," she would say proudly. Our house.

We arrived at the university and entered the main gate, which was lined with tall palm trees. Facing us was a large wooden cross, about twenty feet tall, in the center of a glorieta, and a few yards beyond it was the Mission Church. "Looks like one of the churches in Mexico," my mother said. "*Qué linda!*" How beautiful!

Its Spanish-style façade had carved wooden statues of

saints on both ends and two large dark brown wooden central doors, with two smaller ones on either side. To the left was a bell tower. As I drove around the glorieta, our DeSoto backfired, spewing a cloud of black smoke behind it. I quickly parked in front of a building called Dalia Walsh Hall. New cars with huge, sharp tailfins and shiny chrome fenders entered the gate. Rorra and Rubén pressed their noses against the window, trying to see them. Trampita slid lower in the seat. As I watched the passengers get out, I felt tense. They were all well dressed. Many of the men wore suits and the women dressed in colorful dresses or skirts and blouses. Most of the boys my age appeared taller than I and had crewcuts; some wore jackets. I looked at my pointed black boots and then glanced at my long hair in the rearview mirror. In its reflection, I could see my mother nervously pressing the front of her faded yellow dress with her hands. I glanced at my father. He was biting his lower lip again and his hands were clenched.

"Aren't we getting out?" Torito asked, rolling down the window.

"Not yet," I said, reaching underneath the seat and pulling out the campus map sent to me by the university. I was stalling for time, waiting for the family parked next to us to leave. "I'll be in Kenna Hall," I said. "According to this map, Kenna is on the other side, behind Walsh." I untied the rope that held the driver's door shut, got out, and went around to help my father.

"I am not getting out, Panchito," he said decisively, lighting a cigarette.

"I am not either," my mother said apologetically. "I'll stay with Rorra and your father while you and the boys unload your stuff."

I didn't argue with them; I knew how they felt. While my family waited in the car, I went looking for Kenna Hall to check in. I followed other students and their families who seemed to be headed in the right direction, though a few of them seemed as lost and confused as I was. I spotted a short line of people waiting outside the entrance to an old, gray three-story dormitory, which turned out to be Kenna Hall. The line moved quickly. When it was my turn to check in, the attendant, who was sitting behind a small table, smiled and asked politely: "What's your name?"

"Frank Jiménez." At home I preferred being called Panchito. But my first grade teacher, Miss Scalapino, had called me Frank because she said it was easier to pronounce. The name Frank stayed with me throughout elementary school. In junior high and high school I was called Frankie, which I favored over Frank because it was closer to the English translation of the name Panchito.

"You're not on our list," he said, running his index finger on a long list of names beginning with the letter H.

"It's under the J's," I said, spelling it out for him. He gave me a puzzled look as he checked off my name with his red pencil.

"It's a five-dollar deposit for the key; sign here, next to your name," he said.

I handed him a five-dollar bill and signed. He inspected my signature, shook his head, and handed me the key in a small white envelope. I rushed back to the car, keeping my head down and not looking at anyone.

Trampita and I unloaded the boxes out of the trunk and placed them on the sidewalk in front of the DeSoto. I glanced over and noticed the bulge underneath his striped blue shirt. When he was an infant, Trampita had gotten a hernia. We were living in a migrant labor camp in Santa Rosa that winter. Our parents worked at night in an apple cannery and left Roberto to take care of Trampita and me while they were gone. One cold night, after Roberto and I had fallen asleep, Trampita rolled off the mattress that was on the dirt floor and landed outside the tent and cried so much that he had ruptured his navel.

"Why can't I go with them?" Rorra whined.

"I want to go with them, too," said Rubén.

"Ya, pues!" my father said impatiently. Enough. "Do you understand?"

My sister stomped her feet, turned around, away from my father, and made a bad face. Adjusting his soiled cap, my father said, "Torito, you take Rubén with you and help Panchito and Trampita with the boxes."

"I'll take care of Rubén," Torito said proudly.

"Better behave, *mijo*," my mother said, gently warning

Rubén as he jumped out of the car. Trampita, Torito, and I headed to Kenna Hall, each one of us carrying a box. Rubén skipped along to keep up.

We walked up a narrow stairway to the second floor of Kenna, following other students carrying suitcases, stereos, and boxes. They squeezed past others who were coming down the stairs empty-handed and on their way to get more of their belongings. The dimly lit hallway with dark brown vinyl floors looked like a long tunnel. Loud banging noises echoed in the corridor as students slammed room doors shut. A quarter of the way down the hall we found my room, 218. I buttressed the box on my knee and balanced it with my left hand while I unlocked the door. A ray of light coming from the room's window pierced through and burst into the hallway. Trampita and Torito, who were huffing and puffing, dropped the boxes on one of the two empty beds. I set down my box on the other empty one. The rectangular room had identical worn furniture on both sides: a tall, narrow closet by the entrance, a twin bed with a blue and white striped mattress, and a light brown wooden desk and chair to match and an adjustable desk lamp. "This looks like the one-room cabins we used to live in when we picked cotton in Corcoran," Trampita said, "only it's a little smaller." Noticing my sadness, he quickly added, "But at least it doesn't have holes on the walls!"

"Okay, let's get going. Our parents are waiting for us." I pushed them lightly out of the room. We headed back to the car.

"*Ya era tiempo,*" said my father, irritated. It's about time. "What took you so long?"

"I am sorry," I responded. "It was very crowded." I hugged Trampita, Torito, and Rubén and said goodbye to them. I opened the back car door and kissed Rorra and my mother.

"*Que Dios te bendiga, mijo,*" my mother said, giving me a blessing. I felt my throat tighten and I tried to hold back my tears. My father put out his cigarette and patted me on the back. He reached into his wallet and took out a card with a faded picture of the Virgen de Guadalupe and handed it to me.

"*Cuídate, mijo,*" he said. Take care of yourself, son. His lower lip quivered. "Remember . . . be respectful. If you respect others, they will respect you."

"*Sí, Papá,*" I said, kissing lightly his scarred and leathery hands. Trampita slid into the driver's seat, fastened the door with the rope, started the motor, and slowly backed out of the parking space. The car sputtered as they drove away, leaving a trail of gray smoke behind. I stood alone on the sidewalk and waved goodbye, following the DeSoto with my eyes until it turned right onto El Camino Real and disappeared.

Moving In

When I got back to my room, I closed the door and locked it. The image of my family driving away kept flashing in my mind. I sat on the bed, staring at the empty wall and fighting back the urge to cry. *I have to be tough*, I thought. *This is the opportunity I worked so hard for.* When my father hurt his back and could no longer work, my family stopped following seasonal crops. To help support our family, Roberto and I got janitorial jobs, each one of us working thirty-five hours a week while going to school. My brother worked for the Santa Maria Unified School District, and I was employed by the Santa Maria Window Cleaners, cleaning commercial offices. All during high school, I worked in the mornings before school, in the evenings, and on weekends, sweeping and dusting offices, cleaning windows and toilets, and washing and waxing floors. And although my father taught me that all work was noble, I did not want to pick crops or labor as a janitor all of my life. I studied every night, after work, seven days a week. My efforts paid off. I made the California Scholarship Federation every semester for four years, which earned me several scholarships and a federal loan for one thousand dollars to pay for my first year of college. With the help of Mr. Penney, my high school counselor, I was admitted at the University of Santa Clara.

I picked up the three boxes from the beds and placed them on the floor, near the closet. A wave of sadness came over me as I began unpacking the new clothes my mother had bought for me as a surprise gift for college: two pairs of pants, one navy blue, one black; a couple of short-sleeved shirts; three pairs of white underwear. She saved from her grocery money every week to buy them at a back-to-school sale at JC Penney, as well as my pointed black boots. I smiled to myself as I recalled Trampita's telling me that I could kill cockroaches in corners with them. I taped the card from my father of the Virgen de Guadalupe on the wall above my desk and placed my worn-out pocket dictionary and thesaurus on the top shelf and pencils and pen in the desk drawer.

I finally had a desk I could call my own. All during high school, I had done my homework at the public library and at the gas company after I finished cleaning it in the late evening. As I was sitting at my desk trying to get a feel for it, I heard someone unlocking the door. I jumped up, wiped my eyes, and opened it. Before me stood a tall, athletic, blue-eyed student with a crewcut. Behind him were two women. "Hi, I am Smokey Murphy," he said, looking down at me with a broad, friendly smile and shaking my hand.

"People call me Frank or Frankie," I said. "My last name is Jiménez."

"I guess we're roommates. Hey, I want you to meet my mother, Lois, and Kathy Griffith, my girlfriend."

"Glad to meet you," I said, admiring Kathy's pretty round face and pageboy hairstyle. His mother was short and thin and had a raspy voice.

"I see you have already staked your claim," Smokey said, rolling up his shirt sleeves and checking out the stuff I had brought.

"I hope you don't mind."

"Don't be silly—of course I don't mind." He plopped himself on his bed, which was on the right side of the room, against the wall. "Hey, these beds are pretty good." He lay down on it and stretched. His big feet hung a couple of inches over the foot of the bed. "I wish they were a bit longer, though."

"I don't have that problem."

"Yeah, I guess you don't," he said, turning over and scanning my size. I measured five feet seven inches. We both laughed.

"Kathy and I will go get your stuff, Smokey, while you rest," his mother said in a friendly but sarcastic tone.

Smokey leaped out of bed and put his arm around her. "Now, Mom, no need to get riled. We'll bring our stuff up in no time at all."

"I'll give you a hand," I said, following them out the door.

After we hauled Smokey's things into the room, his mom and girlfriend said goodbye and drove away. I was surprised to see how calm and happy Smokey appeared to be as we walked back to our room. The first thing he did as he began unpacking was to put a framed picture of Kathy on his desk.

"Where is she going to college?" I asked.

"Oh, she's not going to college yet. She's a senior at Woodland High School; that's where we met. She's a year behind me."

"Where's Woodland?"

"Near Sacramento; that's where I grew up. Where's your hometown?"

"Santa Maria."

"Never heard of it."

"It's a small agricultural town about two hundred miles south of here."

"Woodland is a small town too," he said, unpacking a football and a tennis racquet. He swung the tennis racquet as if it were a large flyswatter, tossed it in his closet, and picked up the football. "Do you play sports?"

"Not really. I'm not good at them," I said. "How about you?"

"I love playing sports." He lobbed the football back and forth between his hands and tossed it into the air and caught it. "I played football and basketball, ran track, and played tennis in high school. I'm going to try out for the football team here. What do you like to do for fun?"

"Dancing and listening to music." I was good at dancing. Roberto called me Resortes, "Rubber Legs."

"Me too," he said, catching me off-guard and throwing the football to me. I tried to catch it but fumbled and dropped it.

"I told you . . . " I had no interest in sports. We never followed sports at home and had little or no time to participate in them at school because I had to work.

I saw that he had a portable typewriter. *I could definitely use one of those,* I thought. I had left my old, broken typewriter at home. I had bought it for five dollars from Robert Twitchel, an attorney whose office I cleaned when I was a freshman in high school.

The hall became increasingly noisy and congested as more and more students lugged their belongings to their rooms and became acquainted with each other. I was not used to so much noise. At home we honored silence most of the time because noise irritated my father, who suffered from frequent headaches. I wanted to be alone, but Smokey insisted on meeting our next-door neighbors and making new friends. We met Tony Lizza from Needles, California, and Jim Brodlow from Milwaukee, Pat Hall from San Luis Obispo, Mario Farana from San Francisco, and Tom Maulhardt from Oxnard, California. Smokey's energetic personality attracted students to our room like a magnet. One by one they came, introducing themselves. Within minutes it seemed as if we had met everyone on our floor and a few from the third floor who dropped by to see what all the commotion was about. Pat Hall squeezed through several bodies to get to Smokey's radio. He changed the station to a baseball game and turned up the volume so loud that it grabbed everyone's attention. But only for a few seconds, because immediately they began arguing about what baseball team was the best. Like teletypes, they rattled off statistics on every player and team and had strong opinions on each. *How can they know so much about baseball?* I wondered.

Once we had settled in, we assembled in the hallway as our prefect, Gary, and Father Edward Warren, a tall and thin Jesuit priest who wore a black cassock and Roman collar, welcomed us. Slightly hunched over, with hands clasped, Father Warren informed us that his room was at the east end of our floor and that his door would be open every day from seven to eleven p.m. in case we needed help personally or spiritually. "I am an English instructor, so some of you may end up in my classes," he said, smiling and glancing at all of us. He excused himself and gave the floor to Gary, who proceeded to explain to us that his role as prefect was to enforce dorm rules. He went over a long list of dorm regulations that applied to all freshmen.

"It's important that you guys keep it quiet at all times, but particularly during study period, which is from seven until eleven p.m., Monday through Thursday. I don't want to see or hear boisterous behavior, slamming of doors, or loud playing of radios or stereos. You must have the lights off by eleven p.m. On Fridays and Saturdays, you can stay out until one a.m. I will be checking rooms periodically to make sure you follow these rules." The moans increased with each rule the prefect explained. I did not mind the regulations, because my father was much more demanding. He allowed Roberto and me to go out only once a week and we had to be home by midnight. It was advantageous for us to date girls whose parents were also strict because we avoided the embarrassment of having to be home before our dates.

"If you want to leave campus on weekends, you must sign a form, which I will give to you. And if you leave, you must be back by ten-thirty p.m. on Sunday. There is one telephone on each floor. You may not use it after eleven p.m. Also, you may not have any type of alcoholic beverages in your rooms, nor women visitors, ever!"

"These dorm rules are bad for your health," someone yelled from the back of the crowd. There was thunderous applause, followed by laughter.

"Okay, guys, settle down," Gary continued. "Dinner tonight will be held in the Mission Gardens. The regular dining hall is located in Nobili; it's a dormitory for freshmen girls. Be back by seven p.m." As we were about to disperse, the prefect fired another rule. "No T-shirts, cutoffs, or sandals at any time in the dining hall."

We went back to our rooms, got dressed appropriately, and headed for the Mission Gardens for a special dinner sponsored by the sophomore class. I was struck by the beauty of the gardens, with the palm and olive trees, a wisteria arbor, and hundreds of rosebushes. For dinner we had chicken with vegetables and salad, which we never had at home because my father thought that salad was food for rabbits. I would have preferred my mother's tastier homemade flour tortillas and *carne con chile*. The food was plentiful, and, as a habit, I ate everything we were served—and was shocked to see so much food left on students' plates and then thrown away. At home we never wasted food. During rainy winters in Corcoran, when my parents went days without field work, we had to look for food in the trash behind grocery stores. We picked up partly spoiled fruits and vegetables that had been discarded. My mother sliced off the rotten parts and made soup with the good vegetable pieces and with beef bones she bought at a butcher shop.

That evening Smokey and I made sure we were in our room by seven. A few minutes later, after our prefect dropped by to check on us, we listened to rock 'n' roll music on the radio while we finished unpacking and rearranging our room. I placed my desk against the left wall, next to the window. Smokey placed his on the other side of the window too. We went to bed early because we wanted to be rested for the placement tests in English and math we had to take the next morning and for registration in the afternoon. As we lay in bed, we talked for a few minutes. "I notice you have a thick accent," Smokey said, pulling the covers over his broad shoulders.

"I'm Mexican. But I was born in Colton, California," I quickly added. It was an automatic response. As a child, my father often warned me against telling the truth about where we were born because we had crossed the U.S.-Mexican border illegally. I had lived in constant fear of being caught by the immigration authorities. And even though I now had my green card and felt bad and uncomfortable about not telling the truth, lying about my birthplace had become ingrained in me. "My father doesn't speak English, so we speak only Spanish at home."

"So you'll be able to help me with my Spanish. I am planning to take Spanish for the language requirement."

"Sure, but only if you help me with my English."

"Unfortunately, I didn't inherit the Irish writing talent, but I think I can help you." He paused. "What does your father do?" There was a moment of silence.

"My father used to work in the fields . . . but ever since he hurt his back a few years ago, he hasn't been able to work." I did not want to tell Smokey that my father had fallen into a deep depression ever since he tried to sharecrop strawberries and failed—by no fault of his own. I was in the eighth grade, attending El Camino Junior High School in Santa Maria, at the time. Even though my father was suffering from back problems, he held on to his regular job of picking strawberries for Ito, a Japanese sharecropper, while trying to take care of three acres of strawberries that had been parceled out to him by the owner of the land. My father would work for Ito from seven in the morning until five-thirty in the afternoon, come home, have a quick supper, and head out to the three acres, where he worked until dusk. After a few weeks, the plants became infested with blight, so the land owner had a chemical company fumigate them. The company used chemicals that were too strong; they killed the plants. From that day on, my father's spirit began to die too. And when he could no longer work in the fields because of his back, he became worse. "We must be cursed," he often said.

"I am so sorry." Smokey must have sensed my uneasiness, because he did not ask me any more questions about my father. "My dad is a policeman," he said, breaking the silence. "He's had lots of jobs. He was a security consultant, but also a rancher and farmer until the Depression. Then he worked as a butcher and mortuary assistant until becoming a policeman. He's seventy-one years old."

Smokey's openness made me feel comfortable, so I told him about my mother, who also worked in the fields and cooked for twenty farm workers during the time we lived in Tent City, a migrant labor camp in Santa Maria.

"We must be the two poorest kids in this school!" Smokey said. "My mother is a secretary for the March of Dimes. She also spent a fair amount of time as a volunteer at the labor camp near Woodland, helping poor families. I sometimes tagged along. And while I was in high school, I worked as a park recreation director during summers, serving the labor camp kids. I tried to raise money to get them baseball mitts and bats."

"I am glad we're roommates." I liked Smokey's kindheartedness and childlike spirit. "We have a lot in common." We ended our conversation and tried to fall asleep. Within minutes, Smokey had fallen asleep. I could hear a faint whistling sound coming from his mouth.

I had a hard time falling asleep, thinking about my family. Was it right for me to be here at college while they struggled to make ends meet at home? The more I thought about it, the more confused I became. Then I remembered the English test. Suddenly I felt hot and sweaty and my heart started racing. I threw off the covers and quietly tiptoed to the window to get fresh air. I took a deep breath and stared out into the darkness.

Initiation

Past midnight, I crawled back in bed and struggled to fall asleep. It seemed only minutes later that I heard loud banging on our door. Smokey jumped out of bed like a scared rabbit and turned on the light. "Who is it?" he asked.

"Open up! It's time to get up, you lazy freshmen!"

I glanced at the alarm clock. It was four o'clock in the morning. Smokey unlocked the door and slowly opened it, poking his head out to see who it was. I stumbled out of bed and stood behind him. Standing before us were two tall, muscular students dressed in red and white. They identified themselves as Mike and Jim and said they were members of the Orientation Committee. Mike handed each of us a sheet of paper with lyrics on it. At the top it read "Varsity Fight for Santa Clara."

"This is Santa Clara's rally song," he said. "You have to learn it by tomorrow and recite it on demand." He looked at his watch and added: "Oops, I stand corrected—tomorrow is already here. We'll be generous; we'll give you until eight a.m. to learn it."

"Sounds fair to me," Jim said.

"You got to be kidding," Smokey said, adjusting the bottoms of his pajamas.

"Nope, we're not joking, and if you don't learn it, you'll be sorry," Mike said. Both laughed hysterically and moved on to the next room, yelling, "Go Broncos!" Smokey and I sat on our beds and studied the lyrics.

"I don't have time to memorize this. It's ridiculous!" I exclaimed.

Smokey looked at me, smiled, and said: "Oh, come on—it's not that bad. It's all in fun."

"I don't consider this fun!" I was furious. "We have a test tomorrow!"

Smokey did not respond. He gave me a puzzled look and crawled back in bed. I crumpled the piece of paper, tossed it on my desk, and slipped into bed.

I woke up three hours later exhausted and disoriented. I didn't know where I was. As soon as I saw the ball of paper on my desk and Smokey's empty bed, it hit me like a bolt: The English test! I took off my underwear, wrapped a towel around my waist, grabbed a bar of soap from my closet, and rushed down the call to take a shower. The hot steaming water calmed me down. At home we bathed in a large aluminum tub that was located in a shed attached to the side of our barrack. We heated the water in a pot, carried it, poured it into the tub, and washed our hair with Fab laundry detergent because soap and shampoo were too mild to cut the sulfur and oil in the water.

When I got back to the room, Smokey was sitting at his desk, diligently memorizing the varsity fight song and waiting for me to go to breakfast. He had gotten up early and gone to Mass at the Mission Church. I was amazed at how much energy he had. He was like a giant dynamo. "After we eat, we can go take the English test," he said, glancing up at me and looking at the wrinkled piece of paper on my desk. I knew he was disappointed in me, but I pretended not to notice.

"I'll be ready in a second," I said, feeling tense about the test. No sooner had I gotten dressed than I heard pounding at the door.

"It must be those two guys coming back," Smokey said. I dashed to the closet and hid before he opened the door. Smokey was right. I recognized their deep, loud voices: "Go Broncos! Go Broncos! You know what to do," they shouted in unison.

Smokey began singing "Varsity fight for Santa Clara, Banners of red . . . and white on high . . . No matter how great your foe . . . men, let your motto be 'To do or die.' Rah! Rah! Rah!" At points he sounded out of tune, but he continued, not missing a word. He punctuated the end by chanting: "Go Broncos!"

Mike and Jim applauded and hollered, "Go Broncos!" The noise subsided as they went down the hall looking for other victims.

"You can come out now, you chicken," Smokey said. I opened the closet door slowly, making sure they were completely gone.

"Thanks, Smokey."

"You owe me one, buddy." He punched me lightly on the shoulder.

We headed for the student dinning hall in Nobili for breakfast. On the way I felt lightheaded and had a knot in the pit of my stomach. We handed our meal ticket to a heavy-set elderly woman who sat on a stool at the entrance of the dining hall. From a small table, we picked up a plastic tray, plate, and utensils and proceeded through a line as servers scooped large portions of scrambled eggs, sausage, and potatoes onto our plates. We sat at a round wooden table with a few other classmates. Smokey immediately struck up a conversation with them, but I tuned them out, worrying about the English placement test. English had always been my most difficult subject in school, and I did not test well in it. I felt sick to my stomach but ended up cleaning my plate as usual. I excused myself, rushed to the bathroom in Kenna Hall, splashed cold water on my face, and looked into the mirror. I was pale and had dark circles under my eyes.

I went back to my room and drank a glass of water, then lay in bed and closed my eyes for a few minutes. Then I headed across campus to Seifert Gym to take the test. The old red-brick rectangular building was on the north end of the campus. As I walked in, I was handed a blue book and informed that the test results would be posted that afternoon outside the gym. I took a seat at one of the long, narrow tables set up for the test and nervously glanced around. The gym had a row of evenly spaced square windows along the top of the two longer walls, shiny dark wooden floors, and a basketball net on both ends, anchored from the ceiling. My hand trembled as I opened the blue book and began writing on a topic that escaped my mind as soon as I turned in my essay. I left the gym in a daze, wondering whether or not I had really taken the dreaded test.

When I got back to my room, Smokey was lying in bed, reading the newspaper and listening to the radio. "The Lion Sleeps Tonight" was playing.

"You look like you've seen a ghost," he said, putting down the sports page.

"I hope I passed the English test." I plopped onto the bed.

"Of course you did. It was a snap!"

That afternoon, when I went back to the gym, a crowd of freshmen had already gathered around a large bulletin board on which were posted, in alphabetical order, the list of names of those who had passed the examination. Students whose names did not appear on the list had failed the exam and had to take a remedial English course without academic credit. Students groaned as they pushed and shoved each other, trying to read the list. Some shouted in joy and others grinned from ear to ear as soon as they spotted their name. I stayed behind the crowd, waiting for it to disperse. I struggled to muster enough strength to overcome the disappointment I expected was waiting for me. I approached the bulletin board and quickly glanced down the list, beginning with the J's. And there was my name! I could not believe my eyes. I checked and double-checked to make sure. Even though I was exhausted, I felt as happy as I had the day my tenth grade English teacher, Miss Bell, told me I had writing talent.

At the end of the day, Smokey and I went back to Sefiert Gym to attend a general assembly for all freshmen. The Orientation Committee explained the history and traditions of the university. We were informed that Santa Clara was the oldest institution of higher education in California. It was founded as a college in 1851 by the Jesuit John Nobili and became a university in 1912. I knew that in 1961 women were first admitted to Santa Clara, breaking the all-male tradition. As I looked around the auditorium, I was surprised to see so few girls. I had been used to attending public schools where the number of boys and girls was about equal. When it was announced that our class of 1966 was the largest freshman class ever, consisting of 579 students, one-third of which were girls, Smokey leaned over and whispered, "The odds are not good for us guys."

"Especially at dances," I responded.

What surprised me the most later on was to see how some male upperclassmen treated girls. At supper that evening I noticed that they refused to sit with girls in the dining hall, and later I found out that girls were barred from the football cheering section. The behavior of these students made me feel sad and angry. I wondered if the girls felt as lonely and alienated as I had felt in first grade when classmates excluded me from playing with them because I did not know English.

That night I was so exhausted when I went to bed that I did not even hear our prefect do room check at eleven. I jumped out of bed at six a.m., thinking I was late for work cleaning the Western Union before it opened at seven. I quickly realized I was at Santa Clara and not at home when I glanced over and saw Smokey still asleep.

After breakfast, I read through the graduation requirements in the university's catalogue. The required and recommended elective courses were listed by major for each semester for the four years. Since most majors had the same requirements for the first two years, I decided to take four required courses: Fundamental Theology; Composition and Literature; Logic and Military Science; and History of Western Civilization; and one elective, Spanish, for a total of sixteen and a half units. I jotted them down on a scrap of paper and headed to Sefiert Gym to register.

The gym was noisy and crammed with freshmen trying to register for classes. None of them looked like my friends from Bonetti Ranch or friends I had made in labor camps. I realized this made me feel uncomfortable even though my high school had very few students from migrant communities. Large signs indicating the various departments were taped along the south wall of the gym, and beneath each sign faculty sat behind small tables, giving advice and signing up students for courses. There were long waiting lines for each subject. My mouth felt dry and my hands were cold and clammy. I went through the lines for required courses first, hoping that the classes I had selected were not closed. Luck was on my side. I got them all. I then waited in line for Spanish. When I got to the front, the professor manning the table stood up, introduced himself as Dr. Victor Vari, and shook my hand. "I want to make sure you take the right level of Spanish," he said with a slight accent, looking straight into my eyes. "Do you speak Spanish? You should, with the name Jiménez," he said, smiling and pronouncing my name correctly.

"Yes, I do," I said proudly. He and I proceeded to speak in my native language.

"Well," he said, switching to English. "You must take Spanish 100A, which is Advanced Composition and Reading." I agreed, not knowing exactly what I was getting into. I filled out a card with all my classes and handed it to a staff member standing at the entrance to the building.

As I exited the gym, I was greeted by a sophomore who smashed a Ding Dong cake over my head. He handed me a booklet and informed me that I had to fill it with signatures of upperclassmen by the end of the following day, and that if

I failed, I would be taken to "moot court." He laughed loudly as he waited for the next freshman to come out of the gym. I was not amused. I felt embarrassed and humiliated. I knew it was all for fun, but I thought it was disrespectful. I dashed back to my room, trying to avoid running into any upperclassmen. I stayed in my room with the door locked until Smokey came back from registration. As soon as he walked in, he turned on the radio and proudly showed me his booklet half filled with signatures. "I'll have this baby filled in no time," he said. "How many signatures have you got?" I did not respond. Smokey glanced at me and laughed.

"Did you get the classes you wanted?" I asked.

"Yep."

We compared our class schedules and were disappointed not to share any classes, but we had the same English instructor for Composition and Literature, which made me feel a little better.

Smokey changed clothes and invited me to help create a dummy to represent the "image of the Santa Clara man." It was a contest between male freshman dorms, sponsored by the sophomore class, to build school spirit. My Kenna Hall classmates dressed a mannequin in a red sweater, white shirt, and narrow black tie, and had him pointing to a sign that read NOBILI HALL. I did not participate because I was still upset about the Ding Dong prank. I stayed in my room, missing my family, worrying about the classes I had enrolled in for that semester, and hoping that time at Santa Clara would go by fast.

Unexpected Turns

I woke up early the next morning after having spent half the night awake, worrying about not making my first class at eight o'clock on time. I stumbled out of bed, took a quick shower, got dressed, and rushed to Montgomery Labs, an old wooden two-story building on the north side of campus. The classroom, located on the ground floor, looked like the interior of an old warehouse. It was long and narrow and filled with movable desks lined in rows. Sun rays fanned through its large soiled windows and reflected off the gray concrete floor, creating a haze throughout the room. I took a seat in the front, second row, near a window, and waited for class to begin. I did not know what to expect. The classroom became increasingly loud as it quickly filled with students who were talking and getting acquainted.

Suddenly there was silence. The teacher had entered the room. He was young, tall and thin, and wore a sport coat, tie, and vest. Standing behind the podium, he announced in a strong and forceful voice, "I am Mr. Peter Phillips, your instructor for History of Western Civilization. This class is a yearlong general survey of Western culture from its beginning to the present. This first semester, I'll be emphasizing those ancient and classic institutions which have shaped our modern civilization." I was going to enjoy this course. I liked history and was interested in learning more about the Greeks and the Romans and the Spanish explorers.

"I'll be assigning short essays during the course, and if your paper, which you must type, has one misspelled word in it, it'll be an automatic D." Immediately, my anxiety returned. He proceeded to take roll, calling out names with ease. When he got to mine, he pronounced it "Gymenez." I did not say anything because I did not want to be disrespectful.

I was worried about my history class, but looked forward to my Spanish class, which was held in one of the classrooms in the basement of O'Connor Hall, one of the oldest buildings in the university. Dr. Vari shook hands with everyone and asked us to introduce ourselves. His warmth and genuine interest in students immediately created a welcoming atmosphere. Most of the students in the class were from Central America. They seemed self-assured and used Spanish vocabulary and expressions I was not familiar with. Halfway through the class, Dr. Vari passed out blank sheets of paper and asked us to write a brief composition. He said he wanted to assess our writing ability and knowledge of grammar. Even though I spoke Spanish, I had never written any essays in my native language before, and neither had I read Spanish literature. I struggled to write down my thoughts, not knowing whether I was spelling words correctly. From the corner of my eye, I saw the student sitting to my right writing rapidly and effortlessly. I left the class wondering what opinion my instructor would have of me once he read my essay.

Later that afternoon I attended the course I dreaded the most: English Composition and Literature. The classroom was on the first floor of O'Connor Hall. The worn wooden chairs were fixed to the floor. In front was a small rectangular platform with a desk, and behind it, on the wall, a scratched blackboard. The instructor walked in carrying a bulging briefcase. He was a short, stocky man with short, wavy brown hair and glasses, and he had a small gap between his two front teeth. He reached into his briefcase, took out several books and papers, and spread them on the top of his desk. He introduced himself as Dr. James Quinn and informed us that he was the chairman of the English Department. He lit up a cigarette and proceeded to explain the nature of the course.

"In this course, you'll be writing expository, argumentative, persuasive, descriptive, and narrative essays," he said, taking a puff and placing his cigarette on a tarnished and chipped ashtray. As he talked, the knot in my stomach tightened. My pain got worse when he announced that we were to turn in an essay at the end of every week on a topic assigned the previous Friday. "You'll have a full week to work on it," he said calmly, "so I will not accept any excuses for late papers." I glanced around the room, expecting students to complain or moan like in high school, but no one did. *They must all be really smart and know what they're doing,* I thought, sliding lower into my seat.

"Your writing assignment for next Friday is to comment on and interpret Virginia Woolf's essay 'Life Itself,'" he said, handing out mimeographed copies of the literary piece to the class. I had never heard of the author before.

That evening, after supper, I went to Varsi Library to work on my English paper. On the way I visited the Mission Church and silently prayed for my family. Exiting from the side front door, I passed the large yellowish statue of the Sacred Heart of Jesus in the Mission Gardens and stopped to admire the old adobe wall, which was part of the original Mission Santa Clara. I wondered what the Native Americans and Mexicans thought and felt as they walked these same grounds centuries ago. As I was about to enter the library, I heard the Mission bells toll. I sat on the front steps to Varsi and gazed at the Mission tower and listened to their melancholy sound.

After sitting there for a while, I went into the reading room of the library, which had high ceilings and long rectangular tables with two chairs on each side. A painting of the Mission Santa Clara hung on the back wall. I took out the mimeographed essay and began reading it. I read it several times, trying to understand the point of the three-page work. It was a very brief biography of a man named Parson Woodforde. The essay was based on his diary, written almost daily over many years. There was no mention of his date of birth or the year of his death. He lived a routine and ordinary but stable life. I thought about how this man's secure life contrasted with my own life of constant change, especially during my younger years. I looked up information about Virginia Woolf in the card catalogue and checked out several books on her. I read through them over the next few days but found nothing specific about her essay. I reread the essay a few more times, jotting down ideas. Time was running out. Perhaps the meaning of her essay was that people are happier living a stable and ordinary life rather than living an unstable life of historical significance. Or that it's a challenge to live a stable life in a constantly changing world. On Tuesday evening I wrote the first draft and a second one on Wednesday. I borrowed Smokey's portable typewriter and began typing my paper on Thursday evening, using erasable bond paper so that I could make corrections easily. As I was typing, Smokey came in from football practice. He looked like he had been in a battle. He was sweaty and his pants and jersey were full of grass stains.

"Did someone use your body to mow the lawn?" I asked, laughing.

"Pretty funny." He ripped off his shoulder pads and dropped them on the floor. "I am bushed." He lay on his bed. "What the heck are you typing?"

"The paper for my English class." I reached out to grab my handwritten draft that had accidentally fallen off the desk.

"Oh, no! I completely forgot about it." He jumped from the bed and sifted through a pile of papers on his desk. "Here it is," he said, holding up the mimeographed essay. He sat at his desk and began working on the assignment. I finished typing my essay and proofread it. *This is pretty good*, I thought. I set it aside and began reading for my theology class. About an hour later, Smokey interrupted my concentration.

"I need my typewriter," he said. I handed it to him, then continued reading, trying to ignore the typing noise, but I could not. I closed the book and headed to the library. I returned a few minutes before room check at eleven o'clock. Smokey was wearing his green pajamas and sitting on his bed, back against the wall, reading the newspaper and listening to music. His long legs hanging over the side of the bed looked like two thick tree branches.

"Are you almost done with your paper?" I asked, thinking he was taking a break from writing it.

"I finished it." He put down the newspaper and turned off the radio.

"You're kidding, right?"

"No. It was a piece of cake. Hey, we'd better turn in for the night. It's past curfew."

"I still need to do homework for my logic class." I turned off the light and slipped into bed with my clothes on and waited until our prefect came by to do room check. After he left, I turned on my desk lamp, placed our small floor mat against the base of the door to block the light, and studied until I finished.

The next day, Friday, I attended classes and turned in my English paper. Dr. Quinn did not assign us a paper for the following Friday, so I thought this was my lucky day. I was glad the week was over. That evening at seven, there was a giant pregame rally in the Mission Gardens. The Red Hat Band, a student musical group, played various tunes. I joined the rally, which paraded steadily across campus to Buck Shaw Stadium, where the Broncos were to play the "Aggies" of the University of California at Davis. As we approached the Santa Clara side, we fanned out and quickly filled the wooden bleachers. During the game, four male cheerleaders dressed in shorts, white shirts, and red sweaters ran up and down the sidelines doing somersaults and cheering us on to support the Broncos. I thought they looked silly. I never saw my father or other men in migrant labor camps wearing shorts. I never wore them and even hated wearing them for P.E. in high school.

Santa Clara won the game. The bleachers emptied onto the field as fans congratulated the Bronco football players, who were full of scrapes and bruises. After the game, Smokey and I attended a dance sponsored by the sophomore class. Dancing was like a tonic for me. It helped me forget my troubles.

The following Monday, however, my worries were back. Getting to my English class a few minutes early, I sat at a desk near the open classroom door, facing west. The gentle rays from the afternoon sun streaming through the entrance were suddenly blocked by Dr. Quinn. He entered the room, puffing and carrying his bulging briefcase. He set it down on the right side of the desk, wiped his sweaty brow with a white rumpled handkerchief, and lit up a cigarette. He took a deep puff and informed the class that we were to write an essay on whether nuclear power was good or evil.

"This essay is in lieu of the paper you normally turn in to me on Friday," he said, taking a second puff and exhaling through the side of his mouth. My heart raced as I waited for more details. "You have the entire class period to write the essay."

There were faint moans, light coughs, and a shuffling of papers as students got ready to write. I ripped a page from my spiral notebook and stared at it for a few minutes. I looked around me. Students were hunched over their desks, writing furiously. I thought about the question and wrote down that nuclear energy was neither good nor evil, that it could be used for either positive or negative purposes. I argued that the use of it to destroy human life was evil. Five minutes before the end of the class period, Dr. Quinn collected our papers, gave us a reading assignment, and began handing out our essays on Virginia Woolf.

"You may leave after you get your paper," he said. "I'll see you on Wednesday. As he called my name, I went up and nervously grabbed my paper, lowering my head. I rushed out of the classroom, went straight to the Mission Church, which was adjacent to O'Connor Hall, and sat in a back pew. I flipped to the last page.

There, in red ink, was a large letter "D." My heart sank to my stomach and my eyes filled with tears. I wiped them with the back of my hand and read Dr. Quinn's comments: "Well written and good insights but interpretation and analysis are too subjective; also, too much on Virginia Woolf's life." I felt scared. Maybe I wouldn't make it here at Santa Clara. I said a silent prayer and headed to my favorite class.

Dr. Vari, already in the classroom when I arrived, was engaged in casual conversation with a few students who had arrived early. "Why the long face?" he asked in Spanish as I walked in. Everyone spoke only Spanish in the class, which made it more welcoming for me.

"Oh, it's nothing." I feigned a smile. "I am a bit tired."

"Too much fun this weekend," he said. Noticing that I did not react, he quickly added, "Seriously, if something is wrong and you want to talk about it, come see me."

He began class by commenting on our compositions and explaining common grammatical errors in the use of the subjunctive in "if" clauses. Glancing around the class to make sure we were all paying attention, he explained, "In an 'unreal' or 'contrary-to-fact condition,' a past subjunctive is used in the 'if' clause, and normally the conditional is used in the result clause." He wrote an example in Spanish on the blackboard: *Si yo tuviera talento musical, aprendería a tocar el piano.* "If I had musical talent, I would learn to play the piano." I understood the example, but not the technical terms he used. My concentration faded in and out; the D grade in English kept flashing in my mind. At the end of the class, he returned our compositions.

"You can do better," he said, handing me my essay. I looked at the grade. It was a C–. I was stunned. I felt a wave of heat go through my entire body. "If you need extra help with spelling and accents, please come see me during my office hours," Dr. Vari said, noticing my disappointment and embarrassment.

"Thank you," I responded, looking away. I was more worried than ever. I was not doing well in English or Spanish, my own native language! When I got back to my room, I slammed the door behind me.

"What's the matter?" Smokey asked. He was putting on his football uniform for practice.

"I got a D on my English paper." I was too embarrassed to tell what grade I got on my Spanish composition. "What did you get on yours?"

"I . . . I didn't do that well either." He buckled his belt, glanced at me, and added, "Don't worry about it. Everyone gets lower grades their freshman year in college than in high school."

I was not totally convinced he was right. After he left the room, I went to his desk to borrow his typewriter for my religion class paper. Next to it was his English paper. It had an

A grade marked on it. How could he get an A when he had worked on it only one evening? I had worked on mine all week! Suddenly I became angry with Smokey, which confused me, because I understood why he had lied to me. I felt intense pain in my jaw, the back of my neck, and my shoulders. I took a couple of aspirins and lay in bed, staring at the ceiling, thinking about what to do. I thought about the many sacrifices my parents had made for my siblings and me. They left their homeland to seek a better life for us. My father had worked in the fields ten hours a day, seven days a week, even when he suffered back problems. My mother harvested crops alongside my father and did the cooking and washing for our whole family. Roberto also worked in the fields and missed six months of school every year during the time he was in elementary school, junior high school, and the first two years of high school.

Oddly, the more I thought about my past, the stronger I felt inside. I got up from my bed, went to my desk, and began jotting down recollections about my childhood. I often did this, especially when I felt discouraged. That night I wrote about the frustration I felt my first year of school, when, not knowing a word of English, I had to repeat the first grade.

On Wednesday, Dr. Quinn returned the essays we had written in class. I was surprised he had corrected them so quickly, and even more surprised when I saw the results. "B, Good ideas and well written," he had scribbled on my paper. I felt a heavy burden lift from my shoulders. After class I went into the Mission Church and knelt in the first pew, on the left side, facing the fresco painting of Saint Francis at the Cross. I said the "Our Father" prayer and remained there several minutes, contemplating the mural depicting Saint Francis resting his foot on a globe, his hands touching the crucified Body of Christ. It was as if Christ's sacrifices flowed through Saint Francis to bless the whole world, including me.

The Making of a Soldier

Ever since I was four years old, I felt fear whenever I saw anyone wearing a green uniform. From the time my family and I crossed the United States–Mexican border, crawling underneath the barbed-wire fence that separated the two countries, our father warned us that we had to hide from *la migra,* the border patrol guards dressed in green uniforms. "If they catch you, you'll be deported back to Mexico," he said repeatedly. We managed to evade the green-uniformed men for ten years, but they ultimately caught and deported us when I was in the eighth grade. And even though we came back legally, I continued to feel apprehensive every time I saw a green uniform.

And now I had to wear one once a week during my entire freshman and sophomore years. I had no choice. Like many land-grant colleges, Santa Clara required all undergraduates to take the two-year basic military science program (Reserve Officers Training Corps). The one-and-a-half-unit courses consisted of two hours of lecture and one hour of drills. Every Tuesday morning we dressed in our army uniform and marched in Buck Shaw Stadium on the east side of the campus.

The night before, my classmates and I spent hours getting ready for our Tuesday-morning ritual.

"I know how much you like doing this," Smokey teased me, taking out his army uniform from the closet and gently laying it on his bed lengthwise. I ignored him and continued doing the reading for my Western civilization class. From the corner of my eye I saw him pressing his trousers with the palm of his hands, trying to get rid of the wire hanger crease marks. I put down my textbook.

"You can iron mine when you're finished with yours," I said.

"Deal. If you spit shine my shoes." We both laughed. I took out my uniform, hung it on the door knob, and brushed off the lint with my hands.

"It's easier and faster if you use Scotch tape," Smokey said. He took out a roll of tape from his desk drawer, cut off a strip, and, holding both ends, passed it over his uniform.

"You're a genius; you'll be promoted to general in no time."

"Just follow my orders," he said, "and I'll make you a good soldier yet."

"Yes, sir." I saluted him and clicked my heels. Smokey left to get a haircut from Ernie DeGasparis, my only classmate from Santa Maria High School. Ernie had set up shop in his room on the third floor of Kenna Hall and cut hair free of charge for his friends.

I continued getting ready to pass military inspection on Tuesday. Using an old sock and brass solution, I polished the clip belt buckle, the two small round insignias that were pinned to each side of the jacket lapel, and the insignia of the American eagle pinned to the front of the cap. To polish the black leather low quarter shoes, I spit on them and furiously rubbed them with a small cotton ball until they shined like glass. I had just finished polishing the second shoe when Smokey returned sporting a crewcut.

"Ernie is ready for you," he said. "It's time to get rid of your hair hat." Unlike my classmates, I had long hair with an elevated wave at the front. I hated getting it cut, but the choice was not mine. As cadets we were expected to conform to uniform grooming standards.

And we did. On Tuesday morning every freshman and sophomore male dressed alike and wore a black plastic nameplate on the right breast pocket flap. As we crossed the campus on our way to Buck Shaw Stadium, Santa Clara looked more like a military camp than a university. We reported to the field house, where each one of us was handed an M16 infantry rifle that was about twenty inches long and weighed about seven pounds. We were informed by Captain Glasson that during ROTC activities, cadre and cadets of senior rank were to be addressed by rank and name, and that in the chain of command each one of us would be addressed as cadet and name. We were to use the term "sir" and salute when conversing with or replying to a cadet officer or officer of higher rank. These rules and discipline reminded me of my father, who demanded that we obey him at all times and not question his authority.

We were then grouped in platoons and lined up in rectangular formation. A senior-rank cadet went up and down inspecting each one of us, making sure we had everything in order: brass and shoes shined, crew haircut, and clean shave. If anything was out of compliance, we got demerits, which affected our grade. After inspection we jogged in place for one to two minutes, counting cadence, and carrying our M16 rifles as we marched, following orders: "Attention; left, march; left face; right face; count off; double time . . . " At times when I got confused and did a left face instead of a right face, I heard the senior cadet holler, "Pay attention, cadet!" "Yes, sir," I shouted back automatically, thinking how silly and what a waste of time these drills were.

In the afternoon, we attended lectures given by Captain Glasson or Colonel O'Brien on American military history and map reading, which I enjoyed because I liked learning about the past, but I still disliked wearing the army uniform and going to drill. Eventually, though, having to wear it stripped me of my dread of men dressed in green uniforms; more important, it pleased my father. When I gave him a picture of me in uniform a few months later, over Christmas break, he said, "I am proud of you, *mijo*. You can make something of yourself in the army when you're poor."

A Compromise

Smokey and I got along well except when it came to sports. He read the sports section of the newspaper thoroughly and faithfully every day of the week and had heated debates with Pat Hall, Jim Brodlow, and Tony Lizza, our next-door neighbors, about what teams and players were the best. The debates often turned to yelling matches, each stubbornly defending his opinion as if his life depended on it.

Sports were like a foreign language to me. Whenever these matches took place, I would pick up my books and run off to Varsi Library or take a leisurely walk in the Mission Gardens. My indifference to sports troubled Smokey, but what really upset him was my absence at Santa Clara games. He often tried to convert me into a sports fan, but I resisted like a mule. One of those times was Friday night, the second week of November, a few days before Thanksgiving break. We had just gone through midsemester exams and I felt tired and tense.

"You don't have any school spirit," Smokey complained.

"Don't you care about our Santa Clara teams? Why don't you support them? Do you care at all?"

"I do care, but I came here to learn, not to attend games."

"You can do both. You need balance in your life!"

"You're right; it's *my life*," I shot back, "so let me live *my life*; you live yours. I am tired of having this same argument over and over. Why don't you leave me alone?" I had never spoken so harshly to him. Smokey was stunned. He stared at me as though I had grown three heads.

I was as surprised as he was. We had had this disagreement before, but I had never lost my temper. At home I had learned to control my emotions, especially in front of my father. My hands trembled and my face felt as though it were on fire. We stood facing each other in dead silence. I could see in Smokey's face that I had hurt him. His eyes looked like those of a wounded deer. He shook his head and sat on the edge of his bed.

"I am sorry, Smokey," I said, after calming down a bit.

He looked up and said, "Because you're my roommate and I care about you," he said. "That's why I won't leave you alone. I want you to enjoy life, to have fun." His tenderness and honesty calmed me down completely. He sounded like my older brother, who always looked out for me. I missed Roberto more than ever at that moment.

"I'm really, really sorry, Smokey," I repeated, struggling to find the right words to tell him how bad I felt.

"It's okay." He stood up and adjusted his cap. His tall,

lanky body towered over mine. "Look, let's compromise. You like dancing; I like sports. You come with us to the Santa Clara–St. Mary's basketball game tonight and I'll join you at a dance next weekend. Deal?"

"Let me think about it," I said, glancing at the pile of books on my desk.

"It's going to be a great game." He tilted his head to the side and raised his eyebrows. "We just went through midterm exams—let's treat ourselves. Come on."

"Okay, deal."

"Great! Now all we need is a way to get there."

"Isn't the game here?" I asked. Traveling took time.

"It's downtown in the San José Civic Center. We'll ask Tom Maulhardt for a ride. He never misses a game." Early that evening, Tom, Tony Lizza, Pat Hall, Smokey, and I piled into Tom's white Volvo and drove to the game. It was one of the few basketball games I had ever attended. The old Spanish-style auditorium was in the north end of the city, about four miles from Santa Clara. The main entrance was jammed with students who pushed their way in. We squeezed our way through and managed to find seats on the Santa Clara side, facing St. Mary's students, who sat on the opposite side of the auditorium. They rooted for the Irish Warriors. We cheered for the Broncos. As both teams came onto the court, the noise from the stands grew louder and the stomping of feet made the bleachers shake. It felt like an earthquake. Both teams played well, but at the end the

Broncos conquered the Irish Warriors. All of us, even I, left the game feeling excited, full of energy, and proud. As we drove back to campus, my classmates continued cheering. "Let's celebrate," Smokey said. "Why don't we stop by a liquor store and get some beer?"

"Are you crazy?" Tom, said, slowing the car down. "We're not twenty-one."

"So? I'm sure all of us have drunk before," Smokey responded. "Or did you mean who's going to buy it?"

"I haven't drunk before," I said.

"You got to be kidding!" Smokey exclaimed. "Don't tell me you're—"

"I am not joking," I said, interrupting him. "My father would never allow it." They all laughed. But I had not meant it as a joke.

"Okay, well, it's time you did," Smokey said. Tony volunteered to get the beer. Tom pulled up to a corner liquor store that had iron bars on its two small front windows. Tony got out and waited outside for a potential customer. As one approached, Tony stopped him, exchanged a few words, and handed him money. The man nodded his head in approval and went inside. A few minutes later he came out carrying two large brown bags and handed one of them to Tony. Tony rushed back to the car, looking all around like a fugitive.

"Mission accomplished," he said, sliding onto the front seat and passing the bag to Smokey in the back seat. Tom parked the car near a dark, empty lot on Alviso Street, a few blocks away from campus. Smokey handed each one of us a can of beer and passed around the beer can opener.

I wanted to belong. And I wanted to see what drinking was like and to make it up to Smokey for having yelled at him. But I felt nervous.

"Here's to the Broncos," Pat said, raising his can. "To the Broncos," we all repeated, taking a drink. The beer had a skunky smell and tasted like cardboard. I held my breath and gulped it down. *I don't feel anything,* I thought. We quickly had another round. I guzzled the second can. Suddenly, I began to feel lightheaded and giddy. I laughed at everything my classmates said even though I did not understand everything they were talking about. As time wore on, my giddiness turned to sadness. I started thinking about Tiger Town, a rough neighborhood in Santa Maria, where I had cleaned windows. It had rundown bars and liquor stores that stretched for several blocks on both sides of Main Street. The sidewalks were littered with cigarette butts, crushed cigarette packs, and broken beer bottles. I had to scrub the windows extra hard to loosen the globs of dried spit glued to the glass. Mexican music blasted through the front doors of the bars and a rancid odor filled the air. I liked the music, but the men inside made me sad. Some were *braceros,* temporary farm workers from Mexico, who came to Tiger Town from the local labor camp on Sunday afternoons when work was scarce. They sat at the bar, listening to *ranchera* music playing on the jukebox and drinking beer and staring into the mirror behind the counter. They were all far away from their families in Mexico, just as I now felt far away from my family in Santa Maria. I started to cry.

"Hey, what's wrong?" Smokey asked. "You start out as a happy and silly drunk and now you turned into a crying drunk."

The only recollection I have after that is holding on to Smokey and Pat as we walked back to the dorm before our curfew at one o'clock in the morning. I plopped onto my bed, dizzy and sleepy.

That night I dreamed I was washing the front windows of a bar in Tiger Town. In the dream the clear sky suddenly darkens like a black curtain. There is thunder and lightning and torrential rain. My bucket quickly fills with water, overflows, and spills into the entrance of the bar. The water slowly grows and gains strength until it turns into a rapid and forceful stream, carrying me away, encircled by beer bottles and cans, and dumps me into the Santa Maria River. As I struggle to keep my head above the murky water, I spot a woman dressed in white with long, flowing black hair. She glides along the riverbank, reaching out to save me. I desperately try to grab her hand, but she disappears.

I woke up in a cold sweat. For a few seconds I did not know where I was. My heart was pounding and my head felt like it was in a vise. I took four aspirins and crawled back into bed. Then I remembered what had happened the night before and felt ashamed.

Cervantes Hall

I n spite of the bad weekend, the following week brought me good news. I received an A on my midterm exam in Spanish Composition and Reading and an A– on my English essay. "Good improvement!" Dr. Quinn wrote below the letter grade. I could hardly contain myself. I ran back to my room, feeling as though I were floating on air. I turned on the radio and listened to rock 'n' roll while I cleaned the room.

"Are you tired of sitting around your *chante,* your *casita,* with nothing to do, and getting bored? Are you arguing with your girlfriend about what lousy movie to see? . . . Or maybe you're new to the area . . . Need some exercise . . . Work too much, or maybe just need to hit the social scene in a funky environment? . . . *Órale pues!* Don't be square. Come to Cervantes Hall in Sunnyvale and do the Watusi. Here is Little Eva with 'The Loco-Motion' to get you in the mood."

It sounded like the place to go. I jotted down the name and address on a scrap of paper, stuck it in my shirt pocket, and continued straightening our room.

"Here's 'Are You Lonesome Tonight?' by Elvis Presley. If you are a loner, come to Cervantes Hall tonight and you'll get rid of your blues, man. I guarantee it!"

I had become a fan of Elvis's many years before, when I was in the eighth grade, struggling with the English language and trying to fit in with my classmates. Miss Ehlis, our home-room teacher, asked us to come up with a skit to perform in front of the class. I saw this as my opportunity to be accepted by my classmates who were rock 'n' roll fanatics, and I volunteered to lip-synch Elvis Presley's "Treat Me Like a Fool." I was a hit, and so was Elvis for me from then on.

"Hey, the place looks great," Smokey said as he entered the room, soaked in sweat, after playing a pickup game of basketball.

"Looks like you could use a cleaning yourself."

"What I need is rest." He sat down in his desk chair to take off his grimy clothes.

"There's no rest for the wicked. Remember our deal?"

"What deal?" he said, glancing at me and throwing his sweaty and grimy socks on the floor.

"We agreed that if I went to the Santa Clara–St. Mary's game, which I did, you'd go with me to a dance. There's a dance at Cervantes Hall."

"The name sounds more like a library," he said. "You're not trying to trick me, are you?"

"No, I am serious; I heard it announced on the radio. It sounds like fun."

"What's gotten into you?" he said, looking puzzled.

"I feel like celebrating. I got an A-minus on my English paper."

"Wow! You did better than me."

"Better than 'I,' you mean," I said.

Smokey and I got ready for our adventure. I put on a pair of black polyester pants, a white shirt, and black pointed boots. The trousers fit a bit tighter than they had a few weeks before, because I was eating more than I did at home and not doing any physical work. And the food in the cafeteria was all you could eat for the same price. I rubbed on 3-Roses hair tonic, which my brother and I used at home whenever we went out. I then splashed on Old Spice aftershave lotion and put on my tan corduroy jacket. Smokey dressed in tan pants, a white and blue striped shirt, a navy blue sport coat, and a pair of brown shoes.

"Wow! Those are mean-looking boots," Smokey said, scanning me up and down and lightly scratching his head. I was not surprised by his reaction.

After a quick supper in Nobili, we hurried to the bus stop on the El Camino, the main road that cut across the campus and ran from San José to San Francisco. We knew Cervantes Hall was in Sunnyvale, but we did not know what bus to take to get there. We asked the driver of each bus that stopped if it was going north to Sunnyvale. After waiting and waiting and seeing several buses stop and go, we finally got the right one and arrived in Sunnyvale after traveling for more than half an hour. "What's the address?" Smokey asked as we got off the bus.

"I got it here." I reached into my shirt pocket. "Oh, no! I left it in my other shirt!"

"What! You forgot? How could you?"

"I am sorry." We wandered around the city, asking for directions to Cervantes Hall. No one had heard of it. Smokey began to doubt its existence and was ready to quit and go back. "Let's not give up," I insisted. "Someone has to know."

"Sure, the radio announcer."

"If we can't find someone who knows in the next fifteen minutes, we'll go back," I said, trying to appease him. Luckily, after four more tries, we finally ran into a young man who knew where it was. When he heard me say *Cervantes* Hall, he asked me if I spoke Spanish. When I said yes, he gave me the directions in Spanish. It was his native language, too.

"We're in luck," I said to Smokey. "Follow me; I know where I'm going."

"You'd better."

The sky was dark and cloudy. We walked for several blocks, away from the center of town, until we spotted the green and white neon sign of CERVANTES HALL on the side of the large barnlike building. Outside the double-door entrance, a large, muscular man with long, thick brown wavy hair stood guard. He wore a black T-shirt bearing the name of the dance hall and had a tattoo with a skull and cross-bones on his forearm. Guys dressed in jeans and white T-shirts hung around outside the hall, eyeing the girls and trying to decide whether or not to spend the money to go in. They laughed and joked and swayed to the music that blasted through the doors. Their shiny, long black hair combed back on the side made them look like some of my friends and neighbors in Bonetti Ranch. I felt at home. We bought our tickets and walked in.

The loud, vibrating music and dancing reminded me of the vets dances my brother and I went to in Santa Maria. The live band played rock 'n' roll music nonstop. The lead singer jumped around the stage and gyrated. Screams punctuated the music. Smokey seemed nervous at first, but once he started dancing, he did not stop. And neither did I. We competed with each other, trying different dance moves. We did the Twist, the Mashed Potato, the Locomotion, the Watusi, and many others. We were having so much fun that we forgot we had to be back in our room by one o'clock, and it was close to midnight before we checked the time. Rushing out in a panic, we traced our route back, through empty and dimly lit streets, to the bus stop on the El Camino. We waited at the bus stop for several minutes, but no bus came by. It was beginning to drizzle.

"We're in deep trouble," Smokey said, glancing at his wristwatch and pacing up and down.

"We sure are." I craned to spot a bus. No luck. Only cars

and trucks drove by once in a while. We decided to hitch-hike down El Camino. Since he was easier to see, Smokey followed behind me as we walked backwards, holding out our hands with the thumb up. When no cars were in sight, we jogged. The faster we ran, the wetter we got. Every time we saw two headlights approaching us, we would get our hopes up. Finally a red sports car passed us, slowed down, and stopped. Smokey and I raced to it, looking like two wet, shaggy stray dogs. The driver rolled down the window and asked, "Where are you guys headed?"

"The University of Santa Clara," Smokey and I said in unison.

"Get in. I'm headed that way."

We crammed in, shivering and wiping the rain from our faces. "So, you're at Santa Clara . . . You guys don't have many girls there; too bad. I'm at Stanford," he added. I did not know anything about Stanford, but he sounded like he was boasting. He was stocky with short blond hair and small, plump hands. "I'm on my way to a party at San José State. The girls are more fun there than at Stanford." He continued talking and looking straight ahead, not giving Smokey or me a chance to say anything. His superiority bothered me. He came to a screeching halt at the entrance to Santa Clara. "Here you are." We hurriedly climbed out and thanked him. The ride lasted a few minutes, but it seemed like an hour. I was glad to be back and on time for room check.

Reaching Out

At the end of my long and stressful freshman year, I was thankful for many things. I had learned a lot, made new friends, and had received A grades in English and Spanish, Bs in Military Science, and C-pluses and Cs in my other courses, with an overall B average. However, I was not satisfied and was determined to do better my second year. And now I was going home.

I had not seen my family since Christmas, so I was excited to spend time with them that summer. I returned to Bonetti Ranch having gained knowledge as well as weight. I left for college weighing 129 pounds and returned home thirty pounds heavier.

"What happened to you!" Trampita exclaimed. "Did someone mistake you for a tire and blow you up?"

"It's all muscle." I flexed my forearm.

"Sure, Panchito. You mean love handles." He grabbed both sides of my waist and gave me a light punch in the stomach. Torito, Rorra, and Rubén, who had grown some, laughed hysterically and took turns hugging me.

"Welcome home, *mijo*," my mother said, caressing my face. "Your cheeks are so . . . "

"Chubby?" Trampita chimed in.

"*No seas malcriado, mijo*," my mother said. Don't be impolite. "Rosy," she said, completing her sentence.

From the corner of my eye, I saw my father sitting on the front steps to our barrack. He had been watching us and smoking. He caught my eye and feigned a smile. I felt a cold chill run down my spine. "He's not well, *mijo*," my mother whispered. Her eyes welled up. I went up to him, knelt down, and hugged him.

"*¿Cómo estás,* Panchito?" he asked, after flipping his cigarette butt to the side. His voice was weak. His feeble body seemed to disappear in his baggy and faded clothes.

"I am fine, Papá. It's good to be home."

"Is it?" he asked, straining to stand up.

I did not respond. I knew how he felt about my leaving home. He did not like for our family to be apart. It upset him to see Roberto leave our home when he got married, and he was saddened when I went away to college.

"Why don't we all go in and have dinner," my mother said. "I cooked Panchito's favorite meal, *carne de puerco con chile, fijoles,* and fresh flour tortillas."

"I missed your cooking, Mamá." The cooking at the university was too bland.

As we sat at the table I noticed that the linoleum floor, which we had put together with scraps of different colors and shapes we had found in the city dump, was worn out. The cupboard, which divided the kitchen and dining area, was broken. Roberto had made it in his high school wood shop class, and he had built a planter on top and filled it with plastic flowers. The artificial plants were now gone. At supper, my mother, brothers, and sister asked me endless questions about college, just like they had at Christmastime. Again, I told them about Smokey, my classes, and my professors. My father was silent and distant. As he shifted his body, trying to find a comfortable position, he dropped his fork. No sooner had it hit the floor than he asked for someone to pick it up.

"*No hay naiden que lo recoja?*" he said. Is there no one to pick it up? Torito, who was sitting next to him, quickly reached down to get it.

Seeing this as an opportunity to engage my father in our conversation, I said, "Papá, did you know that the word *naiden* should really be *nadie*? This is what my Spanish professor told me."

"*¡Qué diablos!*" my father shouted angrily. "Are you correcting me?"

I was shocked and speechless. Time seemed to stand still.

"Are you mute?" my father asked impatiently, glaring at me.

"No, Papá. I was just . . . "

"So, now you think you're better than us because you are going to college?" he interrupted me. "*No faltaba más . . . !*"

That's all I needed. He pushed his plate away.

"I am sorry, Papá. I didn't mean to disrespect you," I said nervously.

My mother signaled for me to be quiet and said, tenderly, "Is your food cold, *Viejo*? Do you want me to heat it up?"

"No," my father said, calming down.

I was anxious to leave the table and for the evening to end. "Tomorrow I start work at dawn," I said, rubbing my hands under the table. "I'd better unpack and get to bed early." My father glanced at me and gave me a slight grin. I sighed in relief. He then motioned for me to give him a hand in getting up.

"My back is killing me," he said, bracing himself on my shoulders. I walked him to his bedroom and helped him get into bed. My mother came in with a glass of water and two aspirin pills, which she handed to him. After he took them, he placed the half-empty glass underneath the bed because he believed it kept away evil spirits.

"This is your home, Panchito," he said softly.

"I know," I said, glancing at the image of the Virgen de Guadalupe, hanging on the wall above his bed.

That evening, while my brothers and sister did their homework at the kitchen table, I took a walk around the ranch. The sun was just beginning to disappear.

Bonetti Ranch, like my family and me, had both changed and stayed the same. The dilapidated army barracks that Bonetti, the owner of the ranch, bought after the Second

World War and rented to migrant farm workers remained the same. Looking like victims of the war themselves, the dwellings had broken windows, parts of walls missing, and large holes in the roofs. Weeds invaded the old, rusty pieces of farm machinery scattered throughout the ranch. The pot-holes in the dirt path that circled the front of the barracks were larger and deeper. Bony and mangy stray dogs roamed the ranch, scavenging for food from the three large oil barrels that now served as garbage cans for the residents. The paint on the outside of our barrack, which was about thirty feet wide by sixty feet long (our family lived in half of the build-ing, which was partitioned into two bedrooms and a kitchen), was cracked and chipped, and the front screen door was torn. Our outside toilet, which we shared with our neighbors, leaned to one side. The shed on the side of our house, where we took baths in a round aluminum tub, was in need of repair, and the water was oily and foul-smelling, like rotten eggs.

As the coastal fog rolled in and covered the valley like a large gray sheet, I felt chilly and went back inside and got ready for bed. My mother, father, and sister slept in one room. My three younger brothers, Trampita, Torito, and Rubén, slept in the second room in a twin bed next to mine, which I had shared with Roberto before he got married.

The next day, and for the rest of the summer, I worked again for the Santa Maria Window Cleaners, the janitorial company that employed me during high school. It was the same company that Trampita worked for after I left for college so he could continue helping to support our family. That summer Trampita and Torito picked strawberries for Ito, the Japanese sharecropper. As usual, my old job was routine and tedious. In the early morning, every day, I cleaned the Western Union before it opened at seven, and Betty's Fabrics. I then helped Mike Nevel, the owner of the company, clean houses—doing windows, washing walls, stripping and waxing floors. In the afternoons, I worked alone, cleaning and scraping paint off windows, appliances, and tile counters in the newly built apartments near Hancock College. In the evenings I cleaned the gas company on Main Street and, late at night twice a week, the Standard Oil Company. I worked seventy hours each week, and the money I earned helped my family make ends meet.

Unfortunately, I had little time to spend at home. As time went by, though, I did not mind this too much because of my father. His dark moods, which worsened every day, were quickly dominating our lives. He regularly complained about everything and criticized everyone, especially my mother. Often he stayed in bed all day and refused to shave, eat, or talk to anyone. At times, he locked himself in a storage shed that was in the middle of the ranch where Bonetti kept building supplies. None of us felt relaxed or happy around him, but we continued praying for him and being respectful. When I had free time, I visited my brother and his wife and their baby daughter, Jackie, who lived in a one-room apartment in town. Roberto worked as a janitor for the Santa Maria Unified School District during the week and cleaned commercial offices on weekends.

One evening when I got home from work, a week before I was to return to college, my mother told me that my father had gone to the storage shed again that morning and refused to come out. "Go get him, *mijo*. Maybe he'll listen to you," my mother said, tearing up.

"I'll try." I put my arm around her. She then took two bananas and a handful of Fig Newton cookies and filled a glass with milk and placed them on large plate and handed it to me.

"See if he'll take this. He hasn't eaten all day." My father liked eating bananas and milk products because he said they eased his stomach pain.

When my mother hurriedly opened the front door to our house for me, I stood on the front steps for a few seconds until my eyes adjusted to the darkness. I walked carefully, holding the plate with both hands, until I got to the storage shed. I set the plate down on the ground and placed my ear against the front door. I could not hear anything. My heart was racing. I knocked lightly. No answer. I knocked again more forcefully.

"*¿Quién es . . . ?*" I heard my father ask wearily.

"It's me, Panchito. I've got something for you to eat." I waited and waited for a response. I then heard moaning and boards rattling.

"Papá, are you okay?" The door creaked open slightly and a dim light went on inside. I pushed the door wide open and went in. My father was struggling to lie down on a makeshift bed he had made out of old plywood boards. He was as pale as a white sheet and had dark circles under his eyes and disheveled hair.

"I am very tired," he said, reaching out to touch me. I bent over and held his hand. I then helped him sit up with his back leaning against the wall.

"You have to eat." I brought in the plate, placed it by his side, and peeled one banana and handed it to him. He chewed slowly, staring into space. After he finished eating, I persuaded him to come back in the house. My mother, anxiously waiting for us at the door of our barrack, helped me put him into bed.

"Pobrecito, qué lástima me da verlo sufrir," she said, crying. It hurts me to see him suffering.

"I know," I said, gently placing my arm around her shoulder. I felt a deep sadness. My father had changed so much from the time we first crossed the border.

A Stranger's Gift

I never expected to meet him. I had cleaned his office every day after school during my four years of high school and never once did I see him. His office was on the first floor, in the rear of the gas company, a large building with a main office that connected to a back structure two stories high. I feather-dusted the desks and venetian blinds, emptied and washed the ashtrays, dust-mopped the floors, and emptied the wastebaskets throughout the building. I always did his office last because it was the cleanest and most private. I often wondered whether or not he used it, because everything in it always remained the same. He had his own entrance off a corridor that ran the length of the building. His door had a framed beveled-glass window with his name, ROBERT E. EASTON, in black letters. Entering his office was like going back in time. It had a musty odor and every piece of furniture was old and made of dark wood. The top of his large desk, which sat in the middle of the office, had inlayed gold-color banding around it, and on it were neat piles of yellowish papers and file folders, a small brass lamp with a porcelain shade, and a black rotary phone. His bookshelves were packed with leather-bound books and ledgers. In the corner, behind the door, was a coat rack, and above it hung a black-and-white aerial picture of Santa Maria Valley taken in the 1940s. After I finished cleaning his office, I would sit at his desk and do my homework, because I had no place to study at home. Sitting there, I often wondered who this man was and if I would ever actually meet him.

And here I was, cleaning his office again in the evenings, five days a week, during the summer vacation at the end of my freshman year in college, but still there was no sight of him. Then one Friday evening, Mike Nevel, the owner of the Santa Maria Window Cleaners, asked me to help him strip and wax the floors of a commercial building and postpone cleaning the back building of the gas company until the following day. On Saturday morning, after cleaning the Western Union and Betty's Fabrics, I went to the gas company, picked up the cleaning cart from the janitors' room, and began cleaning the offices on the first floor. As I dust-mopped the corridor, an elderly, thin man with wire-rimmed glasses appeared. He was dressed in a dark navy pinstriped suit and vest, a starched white shirt, a bow tie, and a black felt hat. In his right hand, he carried a walking cane. *This must be him,* I thought, trying to hide my excitement.

"Good morning, young man," he said.

"Good morning, sir."

"I am Robert Easton," he said, shaking my hand. His

wrinkled face and hands were full of brown spots.

"People call me Frankie." I smiled from ear to ear. "I am very happy to meet you!"

"It's a pleasure, son. So you're the lad who cleans for us." He smiled, and his eyes sparkled as he talked. "Are you still in school?"

"I graduated from Santa Maria High School last year . . . "

"Splendid," he said.

"I just finished my first year in college; I am going back next week."

"Marvelous. What college?"

"The University of Santa Clara," I responded proudly.

"Oh, yes, I know about Santa Clara. I've been in that neck of the woods. In fact, I was born in Santa Cruz . . . many years ago, of course. I spent my childhood there."

"It can't be that long ago."

"Oh, it was, son. I was born in 1875, and if my calculations are correct, I am eighty-seven years old. But I am still standing," he said, chuckling. He switched his cane to his right hand and shifted his weight. "University of Santa Clara . . . I remember when it was a football powerhouse back in the thirties. It won the Sugar Bowl in 1936 or '37; I can't recall the exact year."

"It was around that time." I pretended to know something about it. I had no clue, but I felt proud of it once he told me. "Where did you go after you left Santa Cruz?"

"How do you know I lived in Santa Cruz . . . ?" He

frowned, looked up at the ceiling, and exclaimed, "Oh! I told you, didn't I?" He straightened his body, coughed, and added, "Do you really want to know? I don't want to bore you, son . . . "

Before I had a chance to respond, he continued. "Well, okay then. After Santa Cruz, my parents went to Benicia, then to Berkeley, where I attended school." He paused, shifted his weight to his other leg, and looked at me intently as though to make sure I was listening and really interested in what he was saying. I took a step closer to him. "I then went to Cal, and after I graduated from there I worked for a contracting and field surveying firm for two years."

"So, when did you begin working for the gas company?"

"Oh, that's a long story," he said, taking a deep breath and continuing. "Before I got involved with the gas company, I organized the Home Telephone and Telegraph Company. The year was 1907, and two years later in 1909—February of 1909 to be exact—I was one of the cofounders of the Gas and Power Company, which became the Santa Maria Gas Company."

"So, you have been working here for over fifty years."

"Not exactly. I retired as president of the company when it merged with the Southern Counties Gas Company in 1941." He paused, looked away, and added, "Alas, now I am completely retired, but I keep my office and come in once in a while." His voice trailed off, and he had a sad look on his face.

"I like your office." I wanted to cheer him up. "In fact . . . " I was about to tell him that I used his office to study, but I changed my mind. He might not have liked that.

"What were you going to say?"

Pretending to attempt to recall, I touched my chin with my right index finger, looked up, and after a few seconds I said, "I forgot; I forgot what I was going to say!" I laughed nervously.

"Oh, you're too young to be forgetting things." He smiled, but his grin quickly disappeared. "Forgive me for saying so, son, but I notice that your gums are very red. You need to see your dentist."

Instinctively, I covered my mouth with the palm of my hand. "I've never been to a dentist." I was embarrassed.

"Oh, dear! We must take care of this."

I was surprised he did not ask me why I had never seen a dentist. I figured he must have guessed the reason. "Come, I want you to meet Mary, my secretary. I'll have her make an appointment with my dentist to see you. She's in my office waiting for me."

I was completely taken by surprise. Struggling for words, all I could say was "Thank you. Thank you, Mr. Easton." He hobbled back to his office and introduced me to Mary, a friendly elderly lady who was about fifteen years younger than Mr. Easton.

A few days later, Mary left me a message at the gas company indicating that she had made an appointment for me to see the dentist the following Wednesday and to meet her in front of the main office at three o'clock in the afternoon on that day. She picked me up right on time. On the way to the dentist's office, she told me that she had retired at the same time Mr. Easton stopped working for the gas company. As a favor to him, she took care of his personal business and drove him to his office once in a while since he could no longer drive. She waited for me at the dentist's office while I had a cavity filled and my teeth cleaned. She then charged the bill to Mr. Easton's account and drove me back to the gas company. Before she left, I thanked her for her help and kindness. That evening, after I finished cleaning Mr. Easton's office, I wrote him a thank-you note and left it on top of his desk, hoping to see him again. My note was still there the last day I cleaned the gas company that summer.

Making Ends Meet

At the end of that summer, I returned to Santa Clara with mixed feelings. I was glad to leave behind my tiresome and tedious janitorial work and escape my father's depressing moods and strange behavior. But I was worried about him and I was sad to leave my family. They were still struggling to make ends meet even though I had given them my summer earnings. Trampita's salary from working at my old job while going to school, Torito's take-home pay from picking carrots after school and on weekends, and my mother's earnings from taking care of babies for migrant families and ironing for them were barely enough to pay the monthly rent and buy groceries and other basic necessities.

I too had a financial challenge: financing my second year of college. I managed to pay for tuition and room and board with scholarships I received from the university and the Santa Maria Valley Scholarship Association and by borrowing another thousand dollars from the federal government under the National Defense Student Loan Fund. But this was not enough. I had to find a job. My family needed help and I had to buy my books and pay for living expenses such as clothes, toiletries, and laundry.

The first week of September, I moved into room 225 of McLaughlin Hall and registered for classes. Smokey and I agreed to room together that second year, but we hardly spent time together. He was busy with extracurricular activities and classes and I was occupied with studying and work. That fall I took seventeen semester units. The classes and professors I most enjoyed were History of Philosophy with Father Austin Fagothey, who was the chairman of the Department of Philosophy; History of Christianity with Father Bartholomew O'Neill; and Latin American Literature with Dr. Martha James Hardman de Bautista.

The second week of classes I went to see Dr. Hardman de Bautista about being her reader. The door to her sparsely decorated office in the basement of O'Connor Hall was open. I poked my head in and knocked. "Come in, Mr. Jiménez," she said, smiling and placing a book on her desk. As usual, she was wearing sandals, a long one-piece white dress bound at the waist by a wide, colorful woven sash, and a small mantle over her shoulders fastened at the front with a straight silver pin. Her yellowish-brown hair was parted in the middle and pulled back with a headband. "I enjoy having you in my class."

"Thank you, Professor." I was surprised she had already learned my name. "I like our class. It's small," I added nervously, trying to make casual conversation.

"Yes. And everyone in the class is a native Spanish speaker, mostly from Central America, except for one student. Please have a seat." She brought her chair from behind the desk and sat facing me. She had a radiant round face and large blue eyes. "So, what can I do for you?"

"I was wondering if you needed a reader." I proceeded to tell her why I needed a job, without mentioning my family. I did not feel comfortable telling her about my home situation. She listened intently, and at the end of my explanation she asked me questions, in Spanish, about my language background. She then switched to English.

"You're Mexican, aren't you?"

I was amazed that she knew this.

"Yes, I am Mexican, but I was born in Colton, California."

She must have noticed my surprise because she said, "I can tell that you're Mexican by your intonation and some of your vocabulary. You see, I am an anthropological linguist. I study languages."

"What languages?" I had never heard of an anthropological linguist before.

"Currently I am doing research on the language of the Aymara Indians of the Andes. I'm studying the phonological and grammatical structure of their language." She became more and more animated, and her face became flushed as she described her work. "The majority of the Bolivian population, the country where I've done most of my research, belongs to Aymara and Quechua Indian groups. Yet education in Bolivia is delivered solely in Spanish without regard for the indigenous languages, and as a result there is social, economic, and racial discrimination. My hope is that once we create a written language, the Aymara speakers will learn to read and write it so that in the future they will be able to document their own history, in their own language!"

I admired her enthusiasm. "That's very interesting. What you're saying relates to what we're studying in your class about pre-Columbian literature and the Spanish Conquest."

"Exactly! Now, would you be interested in helping me with my research? I need help coding and cataloging the data I collected on the Aymara language. I have it on hundreds of index cards."

I did not respond right away because I was not sure I was capable of doing the work. Noticing my hesitation, she said, "I'll show you how to do it; it isn't difficult. And I have grant money to pay you."

"Thank you, Professor. I'd like to try it." I felt slightly more confident. She then carefully explained to me how she wanted the data coded and cataloged and gave me a key to her office so that I could do the work in the evenings and on weekends. She also hired me as a reader, correcting papers and quizzes for her elementary and intermediate Spanish courses.

My flexible work schedule for Professor Hardman de Bautista made it possible to get two other part-time jobs. I worked in the language lab two hours a day, and on Tuesday and Thursday afternoons I tutored students in Spanish at Bellarmine College Preparatory High School in San José, which was a little over a mile from the university. I worked an average of twenty-five hours a week.

I enjoyed working at Bellarmine, but it was time-consuming and frustrating. It took me approximately forty-five minutes to walk to and from campus, and when no students showed up for tutoring, I did not get paid. So I tried to get another job on campus by taking advantage of my experience working as a janitor. I wrote a letter to the president of the university, Father Patrick Donohoe, suggesting that students be hired to do the custodial work in the dormitories in exchange for room and board. I argued that by having students do the cleaning, other students would be less likely to mess up their rooms and the hallways. I described my extensive janitorial expertise and concluded by offering my services. I never got a response.

I was more successful in marketing my typing skills than my janitorial experience. In high school, I took a typing class and did very well in it because of my typing speed and accuracy. I was so fast that my mother called me a typing machine. "You got fast fingers from picking strawberries and cotton," she told me. I approached a few classmates of mine who were approximately my size and weight and told them that I would happily type their papers in exchange for clothes or money. I ended up with a beautiful light blue alpaca sweater, some nice long-sleeved striped shirts, and some cash.

At the end of the month, after paying living expenses, I sent home any money I had left over. It was not much, but my family appreciated it.

At a Loss

On Friday, November 22, I was excited because in five more days I would be going home for Thanksgiving, which was my favorite holiday. It was not the celebration of it that had the most meaning for me, but the time of the year in which it took place. At school we always celebrated it but not at home. From the time I was six until I was thirteen years old, we spent the winter months in Corcoran, California, picking cotton every day, including Thanksgiving, unless it rained. Usually, a few days before Thanksgiving, I would start school every year for the first time. I would be behind in my studies, but I was always happy to be back in school. For this reason Thanksgiving had a special significance for me.

Thursday night I stayed up late studying for my History of Philosophy course, which met at 9:10 in the morning, three days a week. That Friday, a few of us stayed after class to ask Father Fagothey questions about our readings on Plato's *The Republic*. I was so fascinated by his explanations that I lost track of time and was late for my 10:10 class, which was U.S.

History. I rushed out of Montgomery Labs and headed for O'Connor Hall. On the way I ran into Smokey, who had tears in his eyes. "What's the matter? Are you okay?"

"Kennedy has been shot."

I could not believe what I heard. "Are you sure?" I asked.

"Sure I am sure," he snapped. "Our class has been canceled. I am going back to our room to listen to the news." He turned around and walked away, toward McLaughlin Hall. I continued on to my class, praying that what Smokey had told me was not true. As I entered the classroom, I noticed the lights were off and all the seats were empty. Professor James Hannah, the instructor, was leaning behind the podium, his head down. He was holding a white handkerchief in his right hand and shaking with emotion. His thick glasses, books, and lecture notes were on his desk. He looked up at me, wiped his eyes, and pointed to the blackboard, where he had written "Class canceled."

I stood there in silence for a few seconds and then went back to my dorm room in a daze. As I climbed the stairs to the second floor of McLaughlin and walked down the hallway, I could hear radios in various rooms tuned in to the news. When I got to my room, Smokey was sitting at his desk, glued to the radio. His eyes were red and watery. I felt a knot in my throat. I sat on the edge of my bed and listened to the news.

"Here is a bulletin from KNPR Radio in San Francisco. Three shots were fired at President Kennedy's motorcade in downtown Dallas. The first reports say that President Kennedy has been seriously wounded by this shooting."

I kept praying that he would survive. During the time Kennedy was campaigning for president, my mother favored him because she believed he would help poor people. And when he was elected, she said, "I am glad Kennedy won. He gives us hope." I felt like calling her, but we did not have a telephone at home. Then at about eleven-thirty we heard the final tragic news: "From Dallas, Texas, a flash from the Associated Press has confirmed that President Kennedy died at one o'clock Central Standard Time, two o'clock Eastern Standard Time."

"Oh, no!" Smokey pounded the top of his desk with his fist.

"*¡Dios mío! ¿Por qué?*" I cried out. My God, why? I felt shocked and confused. There was a brief pause. Then the radio announcer continued, "Vice President Lyndon Johnson has left the hospital in Dallas. . . .Presumably, he will be taking the oath of office shortly and become the thirty-sixth president of the United States."

Immediately the Mission bells began to toll. As they continued to ring, Smokey and I left our room and joined other students, faculty, and staff at the Mission Church. We streamed into the church like rivers merging and emptying into a lake. Father Theodore Mackin, chairman of the Department of Theology, said Mass. We prayed and grieved together like a family in crisis, comforting each other.

After spending the weekend mourning the loss of President Kennedy and trying to make sense of it all, I packed a few things to go home for Thanksgiving. On Tuesday late afternoon, after classes, Pat Hall and I got a ride with Tom Maulhardt and headed south in his white Volvo on Highway 101. It was pouring rain. Pat, who lived in San Luis Obispo, offered to have Tom and me stay overnight at his parents' Ranchotel, a motel located on Monterey Boulevard in the tree-filled foothills in the north end of the city. We spent the night in separate Spanish-style cabins, which were warm and quiet and had a comfortable bed and a toilet and shower. It felt like paradise.

We slept in that morning, had a late breakfast at the motel, and spent the rainy afternoon watching the news on television about the assassination of the president. We discussed the possible motives for his murder and wondered if Lee Harvey Oswald had acted alone or if he had been hired to commit the crime. The film clip of President Kennedy being hit by bullets, his wife crawling onto the trunk of the limousine convertible, and a Secret Service agent running behind the car, jumping in the back, and shoving her back into the car before placing his body over hers and the president's kept playing over and over again. Those images became embedded in my mind. They reminded me of the stories my father had told me about the time he participated in the Cristero Revolt in Mexico in 1926. He was sixteen years old and was wounded in the knee and thrown in jail for six months. "Those were tough times," he would say to me. "You could smell death in the air. The fields were irrigated with blood, and men hung from trees like rotting fruit." I could not understand violence. It scared and confused me.

Early that evening, Tom and I thanked Pat for his hospitality and left San Luis Obispo. It rained all the way to Santa Maria. Tom dropped me off at my older brother's house on Donovan Road, which was not as far out of his way as Bonetti Ranch, and he continued on to his home in Oxnard. Roberto and his family had moved from their small apartment into the two-bedroom house.

"What a nice surprise! It's so nice to see you," Darlene said, giving me a warm hug and a light kiss on the cheek.

"It sure is, Panchito," Roberto said, giving me a bear hug.

"It's great to see you too. I hope you don't mind my coming here first before I go home. It was easier for Tom to drop me off at your house."

"Of course we don't mind. I'll drive you home after we visit for a while," Roberto said.

"How's little Jackie?"

"We just put her down to bed. She'll be so excited to see you," Darlene said.

"She's getting into everything, wants to know everything, and has a great imagination," Roberto said proudly. "She takes after her favorite uncle. The other day we're sitting at the dinner table and she's looking up at the chandelier—you know it has light bulbs with shades on them in the shape of drinking glasses—so she says, 'Look, Daddy, the glasses are drinking the light.'" We all laughed and were still laughing when the doorbell rang.

Roberto looked at his wristwatch. "We're not expecting anyone." He went to the door and opened it. "Mamá, what's the matter?"

My mother wobbled in, crying hysterically. The front of her button-down sweater was stained with blood drops. Her upper lip was swollen and her hair was wet and tangled.

"Mamá, please calm down," I said, hugging her. I could feel my heart racing, thinking she had been in an accident. "What happened? Are you hurt?"

"Ay, mijo, no, no . . . it's your dad . . . your dad . . . " Roberto and I sat her down at the kitchen table. Darlene brought one of Jackie's blankets, wrapped it around my mother's shoulders, and wiped her face with a small wash-cloth.

"Is he hurt?" Roberto's voice quavered.

"He's been drinking . . . he got in the car with Trampita, sped out, and lost control and ended up in a ditch near the Ranch. He didn't get hurt, gracias a Dios. Trampita was really scared. He said your dad slumped over the steering wheel and cried. Trampita pulled him out of the car and dragged him home. Your dad yelled at him and Torito and threw them out of the house. I left Rorra, Rubén, Trampita, and Torito at the Ranch with Joe and Espy. Ay! mijo, I don't know what to do."

"He hit you, didn't he?" I said, angrily. I remembered the time my father slapped me on the side of the face with the back of his right hand when he had threatened to strike my mother and I intervened.

"He did, but he didn't mean it, *mijo,*" she said, sobbing and lightly touching her bruised lip and smoothing the front of her sweater. She glanced at me and then looked down and added, "He couldn't keep his balance and when he was about to fall, I tried to catch him, and he accidentally hit me in the mouth with his elbow." I tried to catch her eye, but she turned the other way.

"Is he at the house now?" Roberto asked.

"*Sí, mijo,* but I don't want to go back. I am scared." She started sobbing again.

"Don't worry, Mamá. You stay here with Darlene, Panchito and I will go to the Ranch and talk to him."

The old DeSoto was parked behind Roberto's car in front of the house. We climbed into his car and drove to Bonetti Ranch. My brother and I were silent. We each knew what the other was feeling. As we turned onto East Main Street and crossed Suey Road, I couldn't help remembering how excited I used to get whenever our family returned to Bonetti Ranch every year in late December or early January, after the cotton season was over in Corcoran.

Once we turned into the Ranch, Roberto drove slowly, bumping up and down and swaying from side to side as the tires hit potholes full of water. It was pitch dark and drizzling.

Roberto parked in front of our barrack and took out a small flashlight from the trunk of his car, directed it toward our house, and repeatedly yelled, "Papá, are you all right?"

The stray dogs barked every time they heard our voices. We slowly approached the house and found our father moaning and sprawled in the front yard, near a broken cactus. He had cactus needles stuck on his chin and hands. Blood dribbled from his mouth.

"*Papá, aquí estamos para ayudarlo,*" I said, rubbing his right shoulder. We're here to help you.

He mumbled and tried to smile. His breath reeked of alcohol. Roberto and I helped him up and sat him on the front stairs. A small handgun fell out of his pants pocket. Roberto and I looked at each other in shock.

"What are you doing with a gun?" Roberto asked. My father mumbled again. The darkness was suddenly pierced by a red and yellow flashing light, followed by a siren.

"*Allí viene la chota,*" my brother said. Someone must have called the police. The police car screeched to a halt behind my brother's car and a spotlight was focused on us. I looked down, trying to avoid the blinding light, just as I had when armed men dressed in green uniforms invaded the migrant camp in Tent City, moving through tents, searching for undocumented workers. I felt like the frightened child I was then. The police officers approached us and asked us to identify ourselves. They explained that they had received a call about hearing gunshots coming from our house.

Then one of the officers picked up the gun, which was lying near the steps.

"Is this yours?" he asked in a harsh tone of voice, pointing his flashlight directly at my father's face. His bloodshot eyes were unfocused and his thin, limp body slumped forward. He slurred a response and jerked his head to the side.

"Is this gun yours!" the officer repeated.

"Our father doesn't understand English." The officer made a bad face. Roberto continued, "Yes, it's his gun, but he is disoriented; he means no harm."

"Maybe not to you, but what about to himself?" the officer said. "I think we'd better take him into custody and put him in jail overnight until he sobers up. You can come by the police station tomorrow morning and pick him up."

The officers confiscated the gun, handcuffed my father, and shoved him into the back seat of the police car and drove him away. Roberto and I were shaken. We returned to my brother's house, told my mother what had happened, and reassured her that our father was safe. She calmed down, but she sobbed the whole time I drove home to Bonetti Ranch. That night none of us slept.

The next morning, Thanksgiving Day, my mother, Trampita, and I went to the Santa Maria police station to pick up my father. My other brothers and sister stayed home with our neighbors Joe and Espy. Roberto met us at the station and the four of us waited nervously in the lobby, after checking in at the front desk. A few moments later, I spotted my father dragging his feet down the hallway, accompanied by a police officer. His scuffed shoes were untied and his rumpled, faded shirt was half tucked into his dirty khaki pants. He was pale and unshaven and had dark rings around his bloodshot eyes.

"*¿Cómo están?*" he asked, greeting us with a troubling half-smile.

"*Bien, Papá,*" Roberto, Trampita, and I responded. Roberto gave him a hug and Trampita and I hugged him too. But, strangely, I felt awkward and distant. My mother stood behind us.

"*¿Cómo se siente?*" she asked, wanting to know how he felt. Her tone of voice sounded cold. My father did not respond.

The police officer summoned my mother to the front desk to sign some papers, and after that, we walked out of the police station. We were silent. Trampita opened the rear left door to our DeSoto, and Roberto and I helped our father slide onto the back seat. He scooted over and ordered my mother to sit next to him. She refused. This was the first time I had ever seen my mother disobey my father. She asked me for the car keys. I handed them to her and she drove us home.

A Christmas Break

Confused and sad abut my home life after the Thanksgiving holiday, I found some comfort by going to six o'clock Mass every morning with Smokey, who had joined the Altar Society. But I needed to talk to someone on campus who would listen and help me sort out my feelings. I was managing to complete homework assignments and attend classes, but my mind was not focused on my studies. Father Bartholomew O'Neill, a Jesuit priest and my professor of History of Christianity, noticed my lack of attention in his class. At the beginning of one class, he asked me a question based on the subject of his lecture and I could not answer it. Another day, he had to repeat a question twice because I was not listening. Both times I felt embarrassed and apologized. The third time this happened, he asked to see me in his office.

I went during his office hours. "I've been expecting you," he said in his deep, hoarse voice as I entered. He stood up from behind his large wooden desk and motioned for me to have a seat. His tall and lanky figure, dressed in a black cassock and Roman collar, dominated the dark office. He had a long face, olive complexion, deep-set brown eyes with bushy eyebrows, short hair, and a receding hairline. Students referred to him as "Shaky Jake" because he trembled slightly when he spoke or wrote on the blackboard. He sat back down, clasped his large hands, and rested them on his desk. "For the past few days, you seem distracted and disengaged in class. What seems to be the problem?"

"I am sorry, Father." My face felt hot. "I like the class very much, but I am having trouble at home." My eyes welled up and I felt a knot in my throat.

Father O'Neill leaned forward. "Would you like to tell me what kind of trouble?" His voice softened and he added, "Whatever you say will remain confidential." I proceeded to explain to him my situation at home and the pain and guilt I felt for not being able to help my father ease his suffering or to send more money home. He listened patiently. After realizing how long I had been talking, I apologized.

"No need to apologize," he said. "I can appreciate your difficult situation. But we must not despair. Things happen for a reason and we must have faith and trust in God that things will get better for you and your family, right?"

Yes, but when? I thought. He looked me straight in the eye, waiting for a response. "Yes, thank you, Father," I said after a long pause.

"Good. I am pleased we got a chance to talk." He looked at his watch and added, "I'd like to continue our conversation, but you must excuse me. I have a meeting to go to. Please see me after class Thursday. Meantime, I'll say a Mass for you and your family." I thanked him and left his office feeling better—and grateful.

The next class day, Father O'Neill asked me to take a walk with him after class. We strolled past the front of the Mission Church and St. Joseph's Hall, which was the Jesuit residence. "Lift up your chin," he said.

Surprised, I responded, "I always look down when I walk. I guess it's a habit."

"Well, break that habit. Walk erect and with your chin up, like Don Quixote." He looked straight ahead. "With a name like yours, you should be proud of your Spanish heritage."

"I am proud of my Mexican heritage."

"Good, as you should be," he said, glancing at me and smiling. I kept my head up as we continued walking.

"Are you a member of Sodality?" he asked as we entered the Mission Gardens.

"Sodality? No, I'm not." I wondered why he asked. The only thing I knew about Sodality was that it was a Catholic student organization.

"Many of the leaders on campus, including several class officers, are members of it. Father John Shanks is the moderator. He teaches philosophy. You should go talk to him about applying for it. I'll give him a call to let him know you'll be contacting him."

I was not enthusiastic, because I worried about how much time such involvement would take. However, I agreed to do it out of respect for Father O'Neill.

The next day I received a note through the campus mail from Father Shanks asking me to see him that evening. He was the resident priest for the first floor of Walsh Hall, which was right next to McLaughlin Hall, where Smokey and I lived. When I arrived to his room, number 101, he invited me in, introduced himself, and asked me to sit on a sofa facing his desk, which was scattered with papers and books. Behind his desk was a small grid window that looked out onto the street. His long black cassock fit tightly around his stout and short body. He sat facing me, lit a cigarette, smiled, and said: "Father O'Neill tells me that you are a good candidate for Sodality. Are you interested?" He spoke rapidly and energetically.

"I am, but I'm not sure what it all means."

"Well, let me explain it to you," he said. "Then you can decide whether or not you wish to be considered for candidacy." He took a puff and continued. "Sodality of Our Lady is not only a religious organization but also a way of life. What do I mean by this? Essentially, the keynote of Sodality life is a constant striving for 'more.' It requires a full response to the call of Christ issued through the Gospels. Sodalists are leaders, not followers." He emphasized these last words. "They want not just to live a Christian life, but to live it to its fullest extent. Unlike the rich young man of the New Testament,

Sodalists will say yes to whatever Christ asks of them." He paused, took off his round wire-rimmed glasses, and wiped his eyes and brow with a handkerchief. He then lit another cigarette and asked, "Are you a leader or a follower?"

His question took me by surprise and made me uncomfortable. After a long pause, I responded, "I'm not sure. In high school I organized a Christmas food drive for needy families and ran for student body president and won, but I haven't been involved with extracurricular activities here."

"Why not?"

"I haven't had time."

"Did you have time in high school?"

"Not, really," I said. "I worked doing janitorial work."

"So why did you coordinate the food drive and run for president if you didn't have time?"

I thought about his question for a moment. "I organized the food drive because I wanted to help poor Mexican families in Santa Maria who lived in migrant labor camps, like the one where my family lives. And I ran for student body president because I wanted the kids of those migrant families and others like them to be represented in student government. Also," I added, "a good friend of mine encouraged me to run."

"Let me repeat the question: are you a leader or a follower?"

I did not know what to say. Why was he giving me a hard time?

"Let me tell you what I think a leader is," he said, after patiently waiting for an answer and not getting one. "A leader is one who sees a need to be filled, enlists the aid of others, and sets about filling it in the best way he can find, without compromising his integrity. Most important, a leader has a strong sense of personal responsibility. He assumes responsibility and gives something of himself to solving a problem. Followers, on the other hand, are those who are willing to perform this or that task without becoming personally engaged in it. They attend meetings but see no necessity to contribute; they carry out assignments but never take the initiative; they try to lead good lives but never realize their responsibility as 'my brother's keeper' in the broader perspective of the Mystical Body of Christ." He paused.

Oh, no—he's going to ask the same question again, I thought. He must have noticed my uneasiness, because he smiled and said, "I sometimes ask questions to make students think. I don't necessarily expect them to answer me. That's what we philosophers do—ask questions."

I felt relieved.

"Are you still interested in joining? This question I do expect you to answer," he said chuckling.

"Yes, Father, I am very interested." This would give me a chance to practice my faith and deepen it. I unclasped my sweaty hands and wiped them on my lap.

"I am glad. Now, let me ask you, what career are you seeking?"

"I'd like to be a teacher," I responded right away. Ever since I was in the sixth grade I had wanted to be a teacher because of my sixth grade instructor, Mr. Lema. Although he did not speak Spanish and I did not speak English well, we understood each other and became friends. Mr. Lema was caring and generous. During the lunch hour, he had tutored me in English and I had helped him pronounce the names of Spanish cities in California. When I told him that I liked music, especially Mexican ballads, he offered to teach me how to play the trumpet, my favorite musical instrument. The day I was to have my first lesson, my family moved to another migrant labor camp and I never saw Mr. Lema again; however, I never forgot him. I wanted to be a teacher just like him.

"Excellent," he said. "We select only those who are determined to fulfill the highest aspirations of their hearts. This program combines spiritual and apostolic formation with leadership training to prepare you to make a stronger impact on society. As a teacher, you will certainly have the opportunity to make a difference."

At this point I was certain I wanted to join the organization. Father Shanks continued, "If you are accepted, you'll be asked to serve on one of several cells. Each cell focuses on some aspect of apostolic activity. For example, the Tutoring Cell sends students over to East San José each evening, Monday through Thursday, to assist promising high school and junior high school students who are struggling with their studies and need encouragement. The Amigos Anonymous Cell cooperates with the university as part of a national organization that sends college students to some of the poorer areas of Mexico to work among the people for a summer."

"I would like . . . I mean, if I were accepted, I would like to participate in the Amigos Anonymous Cell," I said. "I already tutor students at Bellarmine in Spanish."

"Fine, it sounds like a good match," he said. "Now, Father O'Neill spoke fondly of you and I know something about you based on our conversation, but I'd like to know a bit more about you and your background." Because he was a priest, I felt confident in telling him about my family and our migrant experience and the difficulties I was having paying for school and trying to help support my family.

"I see . . . " he said thoughtfully after I had finished. He looked up, closed his eyes for a second, and frowned. He then went to his desk and picked up a folder, flipped through it, and said, "You should apply to be a prefect for next year. It will pay for your room and board. Go by the office of the Dean of Students and pick up an application right away. The screening and selection will be done this coming spring."

"I will definitely apply. Thank you!"

Father Shanks tossed the folder back on his desk, sat back down, and said, "About Sodality . . . Well, it seems to me that you are a good candidate for it. I will accept your candidacy, and sometime next year, in April, we'll do an evaluation and decide whether or not you will be admitted. I anticipate no problem, however."

"Thank you, Father. I'll do my best to live up to your expectations." I felt proud that he had accepted me as a candidate.

He adjusted his glasses, smiled, and nodded.

The last day of classes before Christmas break, Father O'Neill again asked me to see him during his office hours. He appeared to be happier than usual. "I contacted Marian Hancock, a good friend of mine in Santa Maria, and asked her if she would give you a job during Christmas break." He went on to explain that I was to contact Margie Williams, Mrs. Hancock's personal secretary, when I got home. He gave me her address and telephone number and told me that I would be delivering Christmas presents to Mrs. Hancock's friends and employees.

"I cannot thank you enough for all you've done for me," I said.

"Oh, don't thank me. Thank God. He is watching over you." He reached into his desk drawer, pulled out an orange, and handed it to me. I did not think it was strange, because other students had told me that Father O'Neill gave them fruit or candy too whenever they visited his office. I thanked him and wished him a Merry Christmas. As I was leaving his office, he said, "Make sure you apply for the prefect job!"

On Saturday, December 14, I got a ride home with Dan McCoy, a classmate of mine who lived in Los Angeles. I was excited to see my family and eager to tell them about my new job during the Christmas break. My hope was that my father would be feeling better and in one of his rare good moods. Dan dropped me off at my brother's house late that afternoon. Little Jackie ran up to meet me at the door and wrapped her tiny arms around my right leg. I picked her up, gave her a kiss, and tickled her. She giggled and tried to grab my nose. Roberto and Darlene laughed. They gave me a warm hug and then looked at each other. "Let's go play with your dolls," Darlene said, taking Jackie into her room and closing the door.

"Is something wrong?" I asked.

Roberto glanced at Jackie's room and whispered, "Our dad left." His lips quivered.

"What do you mean, he left?"

"He went back to Mexico a week ago."

I was stunned. I felt a pain in my chest and was speechless. *This can't be happening,* I thought. After a few seconds, I managed to ask, "Why didn't you tell me before?"

"We didn't want to worry you and interrupt your studies."

"How about Mamá, and Trampita, Rorra . . . ?"

"They're taking it pretty hard, too. Let's go; they'll be glad to see you."

On our way to Bonetti Ranch, Roberto described my father's leaving. Two days after I had gone back to school, after the Thanksgiving holiday, my father had a nervous breakdown and insisted on going back to Mexico. He packed his belongings in cardboard boxes and asked my brother to ship them by train to Tía Chana, my father's older sister, who lived in Tlaquepaque, a small town near Guadalajara where I was born. My mother and Roberto tried to persuade him to stay, but he refused, saying that he did not want to burden our family anymore, that he was worthless. He felt it was a disgrace that he was unable to provide for our family. He then ordered my brother to drive him to the Greyhound Station and buy him a one-way ticket to Tlaquepaque. My brother pleaded with him not to leave, but my father would not take no for an answer. Roberto bought the ticket, gave him some money, and helped him board the bus. "It was so sad to see him go," Roberto said, clutching the steering wheel. "He was crying when he left."

"Maybe he'll get better there." I searched for something hopeful to say. "Tía Chana will care for him."

"He took your ROTC picture with him on the bus," Roberto said. I imagined seeing my father through the bus window, crying and waving goodbye.

As soon as I walked inside the house, I felt my father's absence. My mother looked tired and weary. Rorra and Rubén clung to my mother's side, and Torito and Trampita had sadness in their eyes. They were happy to see me, but not cheerful. "I can see in your face, *mijo*, that Roberto already told you," my mother said, smoothing her soiled apron. I nodded. Rorra started crying.

"Papá left us! He won't come back."

"No, *mijita*, he'll come back. He went to live with your Tía Chana for a few days until he gets cured," my mother said. "He's very sick. Remember how skinny he was when he left? He needs help. He'll be back soon—just wait and see." My sister buried her face in my mother's lap and sobbed.

"He broke my heart," Torito said, tearing up. "I dream about him every night and see him in bed, smoking cigarettes. I can smell the smoke."

"I miss him a lot," Rubén said, clinging tighter to my mother's side.

Roberto composed himself and cleared his throat. "Mamá's right. Papá will come back once he gets better."

"He will," I said, remembering Father O'Neill's words: *Everything happens for a reason. We must have faith and trust in God.*

I looked over at Trampita, who was standing to the side, arms folded and shaking his head. He caught my eye. His dark eyes filled with tears.

"You'd better go home, *mijo*. Darlene is waiting for you," my mother said to Roberto.

After he left, my family and I had dinner, but none of us ate very much. We were mostly silent and kept trying not to glance at the empty place at the table where my father used to sit. Once Rorra, Torito, and Rubén had gone to bed, Trampita, my mother, and I stayed up talking about my father.

"Our dad is never coming back," Trampita said. "He's gone home."

"What do you mean, he's gone home?" my mother asked.

"Mexico has always been his home. He never felt comfortable living in this country. It was foreign to him. He was here, but his mind and heart were always in Mexico. Remember, his dream was to earn and save enough money and eventually return to Mexico with our whole family."

"You're right, Trampita," my mother said, "but I do pray he'll come back."

"You're a dreamer, too," Trampita said to me.

"Because we're full of hope," I said.

"And faith," Mamá added, proudly. "If we don't have faith and hope, what do we have left?"

It Didn't Fit

"If you have a job, be grateful. And never turn down work," my father would often say. This is why I regretted not having a chance to tell him in person that in addition to working for the Santa Maria Window Cleaners, I would be working for Mrs. Hancock during the Christmas break. *He would have been proud of me,* I thought, as I left our house to go see Mrs. Margie Williams, Mrs. Hancock's personal secretary. I checked the telephone number and address that Father O'Neill had given me and called her from a pay phone at the Texaco gas station on Main Street.

"I've been expecting your call," she said. "Come right over."

When I arrived, she greeted me at the door and invited me in. A sweet smell of cinnamon and peppermint filled the air. In the corner of the living room stood a large Christmas tree, crowned with an angel and strung with twinkling white, red, green, and yellow lights. Mrs. Williams was small. She had light blue eyes, short brown hair, and rosy cheeks. She introduced me to her husband, who was tall and husky.

"You must know our son, Ken," he said, pointing to a graduation picture on the fireplace mantel.

"Of course." I recognized him immediately from high school. "He was a year behind me. Where is he now?"

"He's a freshman in college," she said proudly. "He remembers you too. I talked to him over the phone last night and he said to say hi'"

"Please tell him hello for me next time you talk to him." I felt more at ease knowing that their son and I knew each other.

Mr. Williams put on his suit coat, said goodbye, and left for work. For an instant, the image of my father's face the last time I saw him flashed in my mind. Mrs. Williams then explained to me that Mrs. Marian Hancock had given her a list of people to whom she wished to give Christmas presents. Mrs. Williams was to purchase the gifts and I was to deliver them for Mrs. Hancock on the weekend before Christmas. I was disappointed that the job was for only two days, but I was glad to have it.

The following Saturday morning I returned to Mrs. Williams's house, ready to begin my new job. Her living room looked like a huge treasure chest. It was filled with big and small Christmas presents wrapped in colorful paper with different patterns and figures: stars and angels, Frosty the Snowman, starry lights, reindeers in flight, and teddy bears. She offered me a cup of hot chocolate, and after I finished it, she said, "You'll be driving the company van to deliver the gifts." I was glad I wouldn't be driving our old DeSoto. "I've sorted the presents by towns and neighborhoods to make it easier for you. Here is a map and a list of names with addresses."

I loaded the van and delivered presents that morning to places and homes I did not know existed. The houses in Lake Marie Estates, near the Santa Maria Country Club, had large front yards with lush green lawns, trimmed hedges, lattice fences, and flower gardens. Some even had outdoor swimming pools and wide cobblestone or red-brick driveways.

In the pale afternoon light, I drove to Vandenberg Air Force Base, near Lompoc, and left gifts for military officers at the gate since I did not have clearance to enter the base. I was disappointed, because I wanted to see the missile-testing grounds. I used to hear the boom of rockets periodically blasting off from the base when we had picked strawberries for Ito during the summer. They shot straight up into the air through aimlessly roving clouds, leaving a long trail of white smoke.

On Sunday, I picked up the van and finished the deliveries by midmorning and returned it to Mrs. Williams. "My, that was quick," she said, smiling. "You did a fine job. Here is a Christmas present for you from Mrs. Hancock." She handed me a large box wrapped in light blue paper with figures of peace doves. "Go ahead and open it."

I carefully took off the wrapping paper, folded it, and opened the box. Inside was a beautiful dark blue and white

reversible jacket with a hood attached to it. "It's water repel-
lent," she added. This was a perfect gift. I did not have a
waterproof jacket or a raincoat.

"Thank you!" I said. "Please thank Mrs. Hancock for me?"

"You can thank her yourself. She wants to meet you. I am
going to call her to see if today is good for her. Please make
yourself at home." She left the room. I sat down on the
couch and admired a small Nativity set on the end table and
listened to Christmas carols softly playing on the stereo. A
few minutes later she returned and said excitedly, "She'll be
happy to see you this afternoon."

I wanted to learn something about Mrs. Hancock before
going to meet her, but I was not sure if there was a proper
way to ask. Taking a chance, I said, "I am curious, is Allan
Hancock College in any way connected to Mrs. Hancock's
name?" Allan Hancock College was a two-year community
college in Santa Maria where Roberto had taken wood shop
classes at night to make furniture for his home after he got
married.

"I thought you knew," she answered. When I blushed,
she added, "Well, there is no reason why you should. Many
people don't know either." She explained that the college
stood on the site of what used to be the Hancock College of
Aeronautics, which Mr. Hancock had founded and where
pilots trained for service during the Second World War.
After the war, he leased the land to Santa Maria Junior
College for one dollar a year, and when the new campus was

built, it was renamed Allan Hancock College.

"He's a very generous man," I said.

"An extraordinary man. He owns and operates Rosemary Farm and the Santa Maria Valley Railroad, which runs between Santa Maria and Guadalulpe. His favorite steam engine is 'Old Twenty-one.' It's now a museum piece. Have you seen it?"

When we first arrived in Santa Maria from Mexico, I would watch the trains go by behind the migrant labor tent camp we lived in. Roberto and I played on the railroad tracks and waited every day at noon for the train to pass by. We always wondered where it came from. We called it the Noon Train. Could this be the same one?

"Have you seen the engine?" Mrs. Williams repeated.

"I am sorry. No, I haven't. But I'd like to."

She proceeded to tell me that it was located near the railroad offices on South McClelland and suggested that I stop by to see it.

"Oh, gosh, I almost forgot. You need to be on your way." She jotted down Mrs. Hancock's address on a piece of paper and handed it to me. "Rosemary Farm is easy to get to . . . "

I had seen Rosemary Farm from a distance many times. The long cluster of low white-roofed buildings looked like mushrooms growing in the middle of hundreds of acres of green fields. I was amazed that Mr. and Mrs. Hancock lived there. I expected them to live in neighborhoods like the ones I had seen the past two days while delivering gifts.

"I know where it is," I said. "We can see it from Bonetti Ranch, where my family lives."

Before I left she gave me an envelope with money in it for my work delivering presents. I opened it in the car. I was flabbergasted when I saw three fifty-dollar bills. How generous! My father and I would have had to work sixty hours each picking strawberries to earn this much. I wished I could have shared this moment with him. He would have been very pleased.

The private entrance to the farm was on the west side. On both sides of the narrow paved road were small white wooden houses and cottages with flower gardens. They were numbered consecutively, starting with one. Mrs. Hancock's house was number 10. The façade of her house was no different from that of the other houses except for two white wooden pillars that framed the entrance. The rest of it was hidden from view with tall hedges and trees. I nervously rang the doorbell. Mrs. Hancock opened the door. I introduced myself.

"How nice to finally meet you," she said, ushering me in and motioning for me to sit next to a coffee table. She sat down across from me in a high-backed armchair. She had a soft, pleasing voice, a radiant face, sweet almond-shaped brown eyes, and graying blond hair pinned back in a bun with curls in the front. A string of white pearls adorned her collar. She was elegant like a swan. Behind her on the wall hung a floral tapestry with shades of black, brown, white, rose, blue, and green. On a small table next to her chair was a small sculpture of the Virgin Mary and a leather-bound copy of the Bible with gold lettering. I thanked her for the jacket and the job and gave her Father O'Neill's regards.

"I am so pleased he brought us together," she said, clasping her small, slender hands. "Unfortunately, the Captain won't be able meet you. He's ill."

"The Captain?" I wondered to whom she was referring.

"I apologize! I call my husband the Captain. You see, when he was a child, he was fascinated by boats. He rowed a flatboat on lakes at the tar pits in Los Angeles, and when he got older, he designed and built several vessels. Then he got his mariner's license. Ever since, he became known in our family as Captain Hancock. I simply call him the Captain."

"I am sorry he's not well," I responded. "Mrs. Williams told me a little about him. He is an amazing man."

"He certainly is," she said. "He's been a blessing to me. We'll be celebrating his eighty-eighth birthday this year. Since you won't be able to see him, I'd like to show you one of my favorite pictures of him." She stood up, went to an adjacent room, and returned with a red photo album, then showed me a photo of Mr. Hancock receiving an honorary doctorate of science degree from the University of Santa Clara in 1959.

"Wow!" I exclaimed. "I am glad he was honored by Santa Clara." I felt proud of my school. *The Captain clearly seemed a leader,* I thought, recalling what Father Shanks would call a leader. He had certainly lived life to its fullest extent.

"I knew you'd enjoy seeing it," she said, smiling. "Now, before you leave, I have another gift for you," she said. She left and came back with a navy blue pinstriped suit on a wooden hanger. "This suit belongs to the Captain. We would like you to have it."

I was as surprised and moved by this gesture as I had been the time my father had given me his prized Saint Christopher medal for my eighth grade graduation. He had worn it ever since I could remember. I stood up and said, "Oh, it's beautiful. Thank you very much, Mrs. Hancock. Are you sure . . . ?" I took the suit and folded it over my left arm. It was smooth, like silk.

"It would make us happy to have you wear it."

Noticing that she did not sit back down, I realized it was time for me to leave. "It was a pleasure meeting you," I said. "I appreciate all you've done for me."

"You're welcome. Please keep in touch and give my love to Father O'Neill."

When I got home, I gave my mother the envelope. "It's for Christmas presents for our family," I said.

"*Gracias a Dios, mijo,*" she said, giving me a hug. I then showed her the jacket and the suit and explained to her who gave them to me. She looked surprised but thankful.

"*Como hay gente buena en el mundo,*" she said. There are many good people in the world.

When I tried the suit on, the pants were too big in the waist and the coat was too large in the front.

"It doesn't fit," I said, coming out of my room and modeling it for my mother.

"You're right, *mijo;* it's too big for you," she said with disappointment.

Crossroads

The thought of not seeing my father for a long time, even in his worst moods, left a deep sorrow in my family and me. Every day, my sister would wait for him on the front steps and would cry because he did not show up at the end of the day. At college, I stayed awake at night, praying and thinking about what to do: stay in college or return home? I yearned to finish college, but my father's absence had left a void in my family that I felt I had the responsibility to fill. Family always came first, so I felt torn. After going back and forth many times, I made the decision to withdraw from college at the end of the first semester of my sophomore year and return home.

After Christmas break, I went back to Santa Clara to finish the last two weeks of classes. I was preoccupied and irritable. Smokey, sensing something was wrong, asked what was troubling me. "I am just worried about finals," I told him. I decided to let him know about my decision after final exams, because I did not want to bother him with my problems before then. I visited Father O'Neill on Friday and gave him

Mrs. Hancock's regards and told him about my visit with her and the two gifts she gave me.

"Good," he said. "I am glad you got to meet her. She has a heart of gold."

"Yes, she does."

When he told me I looked tired and asked if something was wrong, I shook my head and told him what had happened at home and what I had decided to do.

"Oh, no! I am so sorry. I can understand your feelings." He paused for a while and then added firmly, "But I disagree with your decision to leave Santa Clara."

"But I feel responsible for my family, especially now that my father has left."

"Don't you think that finishing college is also your responsibility? Think of the sacrifices your family made for you to be here. Think of the people who believe in you and contributed to your scholarships. Don't you think you have a responsibility to them too? Besides, remember what I told you. Everything happens for a reason, and you must have trust in God."

"I do have trust in God, Father. And I appreciate the sacrifices people have made for me and I don't want to let them down but . . . "

"Look, son, I know how difficult this is for you, but I think you should take more time to reflect on your decision in light of our discussion. Meantime, I will offer a novena for you and your family."

The more I thought about Father O'Neill's advice, the less sure I was about my decision. That evening, I walked around the Mission Gardens, trying to clear my mind. Was I being selfish if I stayed in college? What about my dream of being a teacher? I thought about how hard Trampita, Torito, and my mother were working to get by. I felt guilty. I returned to my room and struggled to get started on a paper for my philosophy final. I put it aside and went to bed but had a hard time sleeping.

I was so depressed and discouraged by Sunday that I did not feel like going to the first meeting for new Sodality candidates that afternoon. At Smokey's insistence, I dragged myself to it and took an aisle seat in the back of the room and tried to pay attention to Father Shanks. After he welcomed us, we joined him in a prayer for the new year. He then wrote on the blackboard:

What is the meaning and purpose of my life?

The question held my attention because I often wondered why my family and I suffered so much. My father would say we were cursed.

"I want you to answer this question to yourselves," Father Shanks said, pacing up and down the room. "It's not easy, but it's one we must all seek to answer."

He moved to the back of the room, stood next to me, and continued. "Where can we find clues? In our faith and life experiences. Each one of us must reflect on our faith and life experiences and try to draw strength and meaning from them." He paused, placed his right hand on my shoulder, and explained that sometimes we would be baffled by our experiences because they did not come neatly packaged and labeled. He encouraged us not to give up and told us that the struggle was as important as finding the answer. He leaned over and whispered to me, "Can you please come see me in my office after this meeting?"

He walked back to the front of the room, picked up the chalk, underlined the question on the board several times, and said, "As Sodalists I want you to wrestle with this question. Your education and the deepening of your faith here at Santa Clara will guide you in your quest."

At the end of the meeting, several students went up to talk to him. I left and waited for him in the lobby outside his office in Walsh Hall. Through the glass doors to the main entrance of the building, I saw him plodding up the front stairs carrying a bundle of file folders in his left arm. I opened the door for him. "Thanks," he said, catching his breath. He unlocked the door to his office and invited me in.

"Take a seat," he said. He dropped the folders on top of a heap of papers on his desk, sat down next to me, and lit a cigarette. "What's this I hear about your leaving Santa Clara?"

I was surprised he knew. Father O'Neill must have told him. He must have read my mind because he said, "Yes, Father O'Neill talked to me."

"The reason—"

"I know your reason," he said, interrupting me. "Father O'Neill explained it to me. And I agree with him. I think you're making a big mistake. I know that in your culture children are expected to live for and honor their families. I admire that, but you must also think about yourself."

"But you said that we have the responsibility to act as 'my brother's keeper.'"

"Yes, it's true. But in this case, think of the long-term consequences. Don't you think that you would be in a better position to help your family once you finish college and become a teacher? It's a sacrifice you're making now to fashion a better future for your family, yourself, and others like you. Don't you agree?"

"It makes sense." I paused. "I'd like to think more about it." I felt pain in the back of my neck and shoulders.

"I agree. You should take more time to reflect on it. I'm confident you'll make the right decision."

After I left his office, I went to the Mission Church. It was empty and silent. I knelt down before the painting of Saint Francis at the Cross and prayed. Perhaps I shouldn't have mentioned anything to Father O'Neill about it. But out of respect, I had had to tell him. He was my friend and I trusted him. *Oh, it would be so much easier if someone would just make the decision for me!* I got up and sat down in the front pew and looked at the painting of Saint Anthony adoring the Christ Child that was to the right of the altar. The Christ Child figure seemed so pure and peaceful. I went up to the side of the altar, lit a candle, and said a Hail Mary.

I returned to my room and wrote down more memories of my childhood, keeping in mind what Father Shanks had said about finding purpose and meaning to our lives. I wrote about Torito, who almost died from an illness he contracted during the time we lived in Tent City. He was a few months old when he began suffering convulsions and diarrhea. My parents gave him mint tea, prayed, and consulted a *curandera*, a healer, who rubbed raw eggs on his stomach. When he got worse, my parents finally took him to the county hospital even though they had no money to pay for medical care. The doctor told my parents that Torito was going to die. My parents refused to believe the doctor. They brought Torito home and our whole family prayed every day to El Santo Nino de Atocha, the little baby Jesus, until my brother got well.

I put my notes aside and went over the assignment for my philosophy class. We were to write a short essay on one of the works we read in the course and relate it to our lives. I chose the "Allegory of the Cave" in Plato's *Republic*. I compared my childhood of growing up in a family of migrant workers with the prisoners who were in a dark cave chained to the floor and facing a blank wall. I wrote that, like the captives, my family and other migrant workers were shackled to the fields day after day, seven days a week, week after week, being paid very little and living in tents or old garages that had dirt floors, no indoor plumbing, no electricity. I described how the daily struggle to simply put food on our tables kept us from breaking the shackles, from turning our lives around. I explained that faith and hope for a better life kept us going. I identified with the prisoner who managed to escape and with his sense of obligation to return to the cave and help others to break free.

After finishing the paper, I thought about Father Shanks's question and the advice he and Father O'Neill had given me. They were right. I had to sacrifice and finish college.

Soul Mate

I began the second half of my sophomore year feeling less worried about my family and more confident about school. My Tía Chana, who was taking care of my father in Mexico, wrote to my mother, telling her that our father continued to be ill physically and mentally but that, with the help of a *curandera*, he was slowly recovering. She told my mother that he prayed for us every day. Roberto and his wife provided support and comfort to my family by visiting often and helping them out financially. My mother began working in a vegetable processing freezer during the week. Trampita kept on working as a custodian for the Santa Maria Window Cleaners, and my other siblings helped my mother work in the fields on weekends. I continued sending money home whenever I could.

Besides taking seventeen and a half units of course work that second semester and enjoying all of my classes, I found a soul mate who made me feel more at home in college.

I met Laura Facchini in the Survey of Latin American Literature II, taught by Dr. Hardman de Bautista. Laura stood out in the small class because everyone else in it had taken the first part of that course the previous semester and because she was the only freshman and the only one who was not a native Spanish speaker. The other students were from Central and South America and the Caribbean. She caught my attention immediately when I saw her for the first time. She had big brown eyes, a light olive complexion, a high forehead, a narrow, slightly rounded chin, and short brown hair turned under. She reminded me of a girl with whom I was secretly infatuated when I was in junior high school. I always sat next to Laura because I seldom saw her outside of class, and when I did, she always seemed to be in a hurry, scurrying across campus, clutching her books and binders.

One day she came to class a few minutes late, looking hassled. She sat down next to me and opened her Latin American literature anthology to the section on Rubén Darío, a Nicaraguan writer whose poetry we were to have read and studied for homework. I glanced over and saw that she had written in pencil numerous notes in the margins and the English translation of practically every Spanish word in the text. She caught my eye, smiled, and pulled her book closer to her and closed it halfway. I felt embarrassed and looked away. Professor Hardman de Bautista made a few remarks about Darío and assigned each one of us a different poem to read aloud and analyze. I felt nervous and intimidated as I listened to students read with drama and confidence. However, I was surprised that Professor Hardman de Bautista had to guide them so closely through the analyses. This was not the case with Laura. Even though she had a slight accent when she spoke, her reading was smooth and her interpretation impressed everyone, especially the teacher. At the end of the class period, I followed her out of the classroom.

"Where did you learn Spanish so well?" I asked, trying to keep up with her fast pace. A light breeze pressed her floral cotton dress against her slightly bowed legs.

"Oh, I don't know Spanish that well." She glanced at me from the corner of her eye and smiled.

"But you do." I liked her modesty.

"I like Spanish and work hard at it. That's why I decided to major in it. I enjoy learning languages. I guess I take after my grandfather, who studies French and Spanish on his own."

When I told her I was impressed with her interpretation of Rubén Darío's *Canción de otoño en primavera*, she explained that her high school English teacher had taught her how to analyze literature.

"I am still struggling with English."

"I wish I knew Spanish as well as you know English."

"Maybe we can study together." We were approaching Nobili Hall. "I'll help you with Spanish and you can help me with English."

She frowned and said, "Well, here we are. Luckily I

don't have to climb too many stairs. I live on the second floor. Thanks for walking with me."

"You're welcome. See you in class." I opened the entry door and she dashed up the stairs. Maybe she thought I was being too forward.

For the next few days, I did not walk with her after class even though I wanted to. Then, to my surprise, I saw her come into the language lab in Varsi Library one evening. I was working there, setting up audiotape players, signing out audiotape cassettes, and closing the lab in the evenings.

"What are you doing here?" I asked.

"Dr. Vari hired me to help out in the lab. I guess we'll be working together."

This was music to my ears. It gave me a chance to see her more often. And as days went by, after we closed the lab, we spent time together sitting on the front steps of the library, sharing stories about our childhood. Once, I told her about my efforts to pick cotton when I was six years old. My parents used to park our old jalopy at the end of the cotton fields and leave me alone in the car to take care of Trampita. I hated being left by myself with him while they and Roberto went off to work. Thinking that if I learned to pick cotton my parents would take me with them, one afternoon, while Trampita slept in the back seat of the car, I walked over to the nearest row and tried to pick cotton. It was harder than I thought. I picked the bolls one at a time and piled them on the ground. The shells' sharp prongs scratched my hands like a cat's claw and sometimes dug into the corner of my finger-nails and made them bleed. At the end of the day, I was tired and disappointed because I had picked very little. To make things worse, I forgot about Trampita, and when my parents returned, they were upset with me because I had neglected my little brother, who had fallen off the seat, cried, and soiled himself.

"Poor Trampita . . . and you too," she said. She buttoned her white wool knit sweater, looked up at the stars, sighed, and told me about how she helped her parents at their grocery store when she was six years old. The name of her family's store, Hilltop Market, had a sign with the motto "Not the Biggest but the Finest." The customers were people who had moved from the rural South and Oklahoma and lived in modest houses tucked in the hills above the store in Brisbane, California. They would order a chicken every week for their Sunday dinner and Laura and her mother would clean and package it for them. On Saturdays, customers would come into the store to pick up their order or Laura's father would deliver the chickens along with the families' grocery orders to their homes.

She said that her father bought the chickens from a poultry house in San Francisco, and that she would often go with him to see how the chickens were processed. The chickens were held in square cages, about two feet high each, stacked up four or five cages tall. Laura's father would pick out the chickens he wanted, and then the chickens would be delivered to a big, noisy room where they were killed and their feathers removed. All of this work was done by women who wore black rubber aprons, boots, and gloves. Once the feathers were removed, the heads and feet were wrapped in butcher paper and the chickens were put in crates, and Laura and her father would bring them to the store. Laura would help her mother prepare the chickens according to the orders. They would cover the kitchen table with layers and layers of newspapers. Her mother would open the chicken and she and Laura would carefully remove the intestines, heart, and liver. "I used to play with the feet. By pulling on a tendon, I would make them move as if they were walking," she added, chuckling.

"Roberto, my older brother, used to do that too. He would take the chicken feet and tell us it was a rooster's foot. He'd pull the tendon as fast as he could and chase my brothers and me around, hollering that it was the devil's foot. We thought it was so funny."

"Why would he say it was the devil's foot?"

"Because it's a superstition that the devil has rooster's feet when he transforms himself into a man."

"Really! You don't believe that, do you?"

"No, but some people do."

Suddenly I realized I had interrupted her story. "I am sorry," I said. "Finish telling me how you and your mom prepared the chickens . . ."

"There isn't much more to tell. I think my mom was really

proud that she could fill all the orders in time so people could have a nice Sunday dinner." She smiled, glanced at her watch, and said, "It's getting late. We'd better do our homework."

I walked her back to Nobili and watched her rush up the stairs. She and I continued sharing stories every day after we closed the lab. The more time we spent together, the more I appreciated our friendship. I learned to trust her and developed a deep affection for her.

Home Away from Home

My father did not allow my siblings and me to associate with kids who got into trouble. He used to say, *"Dime con quién andas y te diré quién eres."* Tell me what company you keep and I'll tell you who you are. When Laura introduced me to her good friend Emily Bernabé, I knew that Emily would become a friend of mine too. Like Laura, she was a year behind me in college and was majoring in Spanish, and unlike most of the students at Santa Clara, she had a part-time job, lived at home, and commuted to school. We did not see each other on campus often, but when we did, we talked about our families.

Her maternal grandparents, Margarito and Luz Cardona, left the state of Aguascalientes, Mexico, in 1920 with their five children and traveled by train to El Paso, Texas, and settled in Redwood City, California. They came to the United States to work and seek a better life for their children. Being the oldest child, Emily's mother, Juanita, had to drop out of the eighth grade to help her parents support the family. She eventually married and had two children: Gilbert and Emily.

Gilbert was four years older than Emily. In the early 1950s Emily's mother became a single parent and struggled to make ends meet, working in the Del Monte Cannery and Stokeley's Packing House in San José. She often worked two and three jobs during the summer months so Emily and her brother could attend Catholic schools.

One Friday, Emily and I talked about painful experiences we had in grammar school. I told her how I had failed first grade because I did not know English well enough and how I was teased because of my accent, and how Roberto and I were not allowed to speak Spanish in school, even though it was the only language we knew.

Emily told me that she was never allowed to speak Spanish in school either. Her mother spoke English as well as Spanish, so Emily knew English when she started school. However, she felt hurt and insulted whenever kids pointed out the dark color of her skin. I told her that my mother thought that people who had prejudices were ignorant and blinded by the devil. Emily and I agreed—ignorance was the devil.

Emily invited Laura and me to her house for dinner that weekend. Saturday afternoon, she picked us up in front of McLaughlin Hall in her old blue Volkswagen and drove us to her house, which was about ten minutes from the university.

"I am so glad to see you again, Laura. *Bien venidos*," Juanita said, welcoming us. It's so nice meet you, Panchito."

"I am glad to meet you too, Mrs. Bernabé."

She had curly, short black hair, a round face, brown sparkly eyes, and a small, wide nose. Her gentleness reminded me of my mother's warmth. The small living room was sparsely furnished and neat, with family pictures on the walls. We sat at the kitchen table and ate my favorite meal: refried beans, rice, *carne con chile,* and freshly made flour tortillas. From the corner of my eye, I saw a *molcajete,* a stone mortar, on the kitchen counter. On the wall above it hung a Mexican calendar. I felt right at home.

I visited Emily and her mother several times after that, and each time I felt as if I were with my own family.

Paisano

I saw Rafael Hernández for the first time one afternoon on my way to class. He was in the corridor on the second floor of McLaughlin Hall emptying a trash can into a cleaning cart, which held a trash bag, a sponge, and toilet supplies. It reminded me of the cart I used when I cleaned the gas company in Santa Maria. "Hello," I said. He grinned and nodded. He had coppery skin, brilliant dark eyes, high cheekbones, and thick, straight black hair. After that day, we exchanged greetings every time we saw each other, but we did not meet until one Sunday morning at the Mission Church.

I was attending Mass when I spotted him sitting a few pews in front of me. After the service ended, I went up to him and introduced myself. He recognized me but seemed tense and reserved. When I spoke in Spanish and told him that my father was from the state of Jalisco in Mexico, his eyes lit up.

"*Nuestros padres son paisanos,*" he said, smiling. Our fathers are fellow countrymen. "My father was born in Lagos de Moreno."

We strolled through the Mission Gardens, talking in Spanish about our families and work. He said that he had recently started working as a janitor at Santa Clara after having worked in the fields, picking fruits and vegetables in the San Joaquin Valley and Salinas. When I told him that I too had worked in the fields and as a janitor, he was surprised. The lines etched on his brow became more pronounced. "How did you manage to go to college?" he asked.

"I got some scholarships and loans. And my family has made many sacrifices for me to be here."

"You are so lucky to have those opportunities here," he said. "It's a lot more difficult in Mexico."

When we arrived at my dormitory, he pointed out that he lived only two blocks away, in a small house. From that day on, we chatted a few minutes every time we ran into each other.

He was born and raised in Paredones, a tiny village near Guadalajara, Mexico. When his father died, he dropped out of school and took a job to help his widowed mother make ends meet. Rafael and his mother took a long bus ride every day to go to work for a wealthy rancher. She worked as a maid and he as a ranch hand. Eventually, Rafael got married and started his own family. He had two children, a boy and a girl. When he lost his job and his wife became gravely ill, he decided to leave his wife and two children under his mother's care and head for the United States, hoping to find work to pay for his wife's medical expenses and support his family. He took a bus to Juárez and, with the help of a *coyote*, crossed the border to El Paso. From there he made his way to the San Joaquin Valley, to Salinas, and then to Santa Clara.

Several weeks after we first met, he invited me to his home, which was a rented room in a small white wooden house located on a corner street. He said he had something to tell me and a gift to give me. The entrance was on the south end of the white wooden structure. *"Aquí tiene su casa,"* he said, welcoming me and offering a wooden chair for me to sit on. The room had no windows and a sweaty and salty odor. In the back corner was a small kitchen table. On top of it were an electric hot plate and two dented pots and a pan. Underneath it was an aluminum washbasin, a stack of canned foods, soft drinks, and a box of macaroni. A calendar with a picture of the Virgen de Guadalupe hung above his cot, which was pushed against the wall. A wooden crate full of books and magazines with a Del Monte label on it was next to his bed. He sat on a three-legged wooden stool, to the right of the entrance. As usual, he wore khaki pants and a blue long-sleeve cotton shirt, slightly open at the neck. "I am glad you came. I couldn't leave without saying goodbye to you."

"Leaving, why?" I was shocked and disappointed.

"I am going back to Paredones. I miss my family and my country. I've been sending money home every month to pay the doctor and, thank God, my wife has recovered. Life is too hard for us in this country. There are people here who think that we Mexicans are no more than animals. In Texas I saw signs in restaurants that said, 'No Mexicans or Dogs Allowed.' It's humiliating."

"Yes, it is." His words reminded me of Díaz, a labor contractor I had known. He tried to force a *bracero* to pull a plow like an ox, and when he refused, the contractor had him deported back to Mexico.

"But we endure for the sake of our children," he said, with a spark in his eyes. He crossed himself three times and added: "And thanks to the Virgen de Guadalupe and the good Jesuit priests at Santa Clara, I am now able to return home and be with my family."

I was happy for him and glad his wife was fine now but sad to see him go. He stood up, went to the Del Monte box and picked up a worn book, and handed it to me as a gift.

"Thank you very much," I said, glancing at the title, *La patria perdida,* wondering why the author named it *The Lost Homeland.*

"A good friend of mine gave me this novel and begged me not to come to the United States. She said her father died in the desert trying to cross the border, and she didn't want me to have the same fate. The author lived in San Antonio, Texas, a few years. And while he lived there, he experienced discrimination and, like me, he missed his homeland. He wrote about this in his novel, so when you read it, think of me."

"I will. It's a great gift. Thanks again," I said. We said

goodbye and promised each other to keep in touch. I never saw or heard from him again, but I felt grateful for having known him. He helped me to better understand my father's own yearning for his homeland and his long-held dream of returning to Mexico with our whole family.

In a Cell

I returned to Santa Clara in the fall to begin my third year in college. I had spent the summer in Santa Maria living with my family, missing my father, but keeping busy by working full-time for the Southern Counties Gas Company doing odd jobs: cleaning the yard, helping in the warehouse, and painting gas meters in various locations, from Lompoc in the south to Paso Robles in the north. On weekends I worked with my brother doing janitorial work for the Santa Maria Window Cleaners. Unlike my two previous years, I began my junior year without having to borrow money to attend school. I applied for and got a prefect job, which paid for my room and board, and received scholarships from Santa Clara that covered tuition. I continued working on campus as a research assistant and reader for Dr. Hardman de Bautista and as a language lab monitor.

I moved into Walsh Hall, room 102, which was adjacent to Father John Shanks's residence. My new roommate, James Clark, was a graduate student preparing to become a high school teacher. He was small and thin and had a narrow face, short brown hair parted to the side, and a sweet, high-pitched voice. He was meticulously clean and neat. Nothing of his was ever out of place. Every day he went to bed at eleven and got up at six a.m. On Sunday mornings he often went home, right after eight o'clock Mass, to visit his family in Healdsburg. Like Smokey, he was a sports fanatic. He regularly listened to baseball games on the radio and commented on every player. When a fielder made an error, James shouted at him and wigwagged his arms, making him look like a fragile windmill. As prefects, he and I shared duties, enforcing dorm rules, but we did not socialize together. We saw each other in the evenings and sometimes on weekends, but hardly ever when sports games were broadcast on the radio.

Besides having a different roommate and an additional job that year, I entered my junior year under a new class schedule called the Santa Clara Plan, which was a switch from the semester system to a modified quarter system. Juniors and seniors took only three five-unit classes. This new plan made it easier for me to concentrate on fewer subjects at a time and to get more involved in Sodality.

As a member of Sodality, I decided to participate in the Amigos Anonymous Cell, which was one of three cells I could join in the organization. I helped prepare college students to work in the poorer areas of Mexico during the summer by tutoring them in the Spanish language and culture. Periodically, Sodalists broke into smaller cells to discuss various contemporary issues. I attended a cell meeting on the topic of interfaith marriages one Wednesday afternoon. The discussion had already started when I entered the meeting room. There were about eleven students in the group, most of them male seniors, sitting around a worn wooden rectangular table. I pulled out a chair and sat behind a student who was sitting at one end of the table. As usual, I kept quiet and listened. I did not feel comfortable speaking in groups, especially in English. Students calmly discussed the pros and cons of marrying someone from a different religious faith. There was general agreement that it would be preferable to marry someone who had the same religious beliefs.

The relaxed discussion turned into a heated debate about interracial marriages and prejudice, which brought painful memories. Roberto's girlfriend in high school had not been allowed by her parents to date him because he was Mexican. I remembered the sorrow and humiliation in his face when he first told me about it.

"There's discrimination in our society," one student argued. "I am glad President Johnson signed the Civil Rights Act, outlawing discrimination."

"Laws can't end discrimination," another student countered.

"Of course not, but laws can control harmful acts."

"Not always—look at what happened to Michael Schwerner this past summer. He was killed by the Ku Klux Klan because he got involved in the civil rights movement.

He was helping Mississippi blacks to register to vote. Besides, what is lawful is not always right. For example, slavery was legal in our country for many years. Was it right?"

"Are you saying that the Civil Rights Act is not a good thing?"

"No, what I am saying is that we sometimes make bad laws."

He turned red, looked down, cleared his throat, and said, "I don't have any prejudices, but it bothers me a lot when we do things for fun and people get upset." He went on to describe how some college students had chased down a couple of Mexican high school kids and jokingly threatened to cut off their long hair. They were accused of being prejudiced. "They were just having a good time," he added.

I could not believe my ears. I glanced around. Some students frowned; others raised their eyebrows and shook their heads.

Joe, a tall and gangly senior, stood up and said, "Let's be honest here. I don't think any of us thinks it's a good idea to have interracial marriages. I wouldn't want my sister or daughter to marry a Mexican . . . "

I felt as if I had been kicked in the stomach. I tuned out immediately. I tightened my lips, stood up, and stormed out of the room. Halfway down the hall, I heard Joe running behind me, yelling, "Frank, Frank, wait. I'm sorry." I stopped and faced him. "I am very sorry," he said frantically. "I didn't know you were Mexican."

"You should feel sorry for yourself." I glared at him. "You're the one who has the problem." I raised my voice and repeated, "You should feel sorry for yourself." He looked stunned and confused. I turned around and walked off.

For a long time after that, I wondered how many others felt the way he did but hid those feelings from me because they knew I was Mexican.

A Secret Revealed

I had to tell Laura the truth. I could no longer keep my secret from her. After we had closed the language lab one evening, we sat side by side on the front steps of Varsi Hall, watching in silence the tiny golden fish in a small, round pond a few feet away. A white weather-beaten statue of a child, poised in the middle of it, shouldered a vase from which a thin stream of water poured into the pond. Once in a while we would glance at each other and smile. "What are you thinking?" Laura asked.

"I have something important I want to tell you," I said. "Do you want to get a cup of coffee?"

My idea was to go away from campus because I didn't want anyone else to hear what I was about to tell her. We strolled down Franklin Street, looking for a coffee shop. We passed Wade's Mission Pharmacy, the University Electric Company, the Santa Clara Movie Theater, the Genova Delicatessen. No luck. We finally found one on Sherman Street. I opened the door for her. She smiled. We sat at a small table, across from each other, and ordered two cups of coffee. It took all the courage I had to begin to tell her my secret. "I've wanted to tell you this for a long time."

"What is it?" She frowned slightly.

"I was not born in this country. I was born in Mexico," I blurted out. There, I had said it.

"Is that it?" She gave me a puzzled look. "Neither was most of my family."

She proceeded to tell me that her maternal grandfather, Arrigo Descalzi, had emigrated to the United States from Sestre Levante, a small town in the northern part of Italy. Being quite adventuresome, he boarded a ship at the age of sixteen and landed in New York, passing through Ellis Island. He didn't know a word of English and ended up in California working on farms and selling vegetables from a horse-drawn wagon. He met and married Caterina Zunino, who also came from Italy. She worked as a chambermaid in San Francisco. Laura's paternal grandparents, Ferdinando and Rosa, also born in Italy, settled in San Francisco and ran a small business.

Laura paused, and said, "Tell me more about yourself, or is that all you wanted to tell me?"

Feeling more at ease, I told her about our family crossing the border illegally when I was four years old and about being caught by the Border Patrol and deported back to Mexico ten years later. I described my family life in the years that followed, including my father's leaving. It was like a personal confession. I talked for a long time, and when I finally stopped, Laura gave me a sweet smile and gently placed her right hand over mine. I felt peaceful inside. After a long period of silence, I asked, "Do you speak Italian?"

"Yes, in fact, I spoke more Italian at home than English. You see, my mother passed away when I was nine years old. She died from multiple sclerosis . . ." Laura paused. Her eyes filled with tears and her hands trembled as she buttoned her white sweater, trying to buy time to compose herself. "So . . . I was raised by my maternal grandparents, who spoke only Italian at home."

"I am sorry. She must have been very young."

"She was only thirty-two years old. No one knew what was wrong with her when she first got sick. She slowly began to lose her eyesight and control of her legs until she could no longer see or walk. Eventually she became bedridden. I would sit on the edge of her bed and read out loud to her and my younger sister, Lynn, every day when I got home from school. We had no medical insurance, so my Dad worked all day running the grocery store in Brisbane, the one I told you about, and in the evenings he played the accordion at nightclubs or, on weekends, at weddings to make ends meet. Poor Dad—his hair turned completely gray and he lost a lot of weight. I felt so helpless." The waitress came by and interrupted her.

"More coffee?"

"No, thank you." She looked startled.

"I'm sorry. I didn't mean to go on and on," she said when the waitress had left.

"It's okay. Thank you for telling me," I said awkwardly. I was at a loss for words to comfort her.

She collected herself and added proudly, "So I grew up speaking Italian at home. In fact, not only did we speak Italian, but we lived in an Italian neighborhood, shopped at Italian-owned businesses, and ate Italian food most of the time."

I admired her feelings about her Italian heritage. I was proud of my heritage too.

"What about your ancestors?" she asked.

I told her how my grandparents were poor peasants from Los Altos de Jalisco. My paternal grandfather, Hilario, was a small farmer who died in 1910, when my father was a few months old. For the first eleven years of his life, my father, who was the youngest of sixteen children, was raised by my grandmother, Estafanía, who was part Huichol Indian and very religious. He spent the next four years, living here and there a few months at a time, with his older brothers and sisters who were married. He never attended school, and by the time he was fifteen, he was on his own working as a ranch hand in El Rancho Blanco. At the age of twenty-seven, he met and married my mother in Tlaquepaque. She was sixteen. My maternal grandfather, Salvador Hernández, was an *arriero*, a mule driver. He married my grandmother, Concepción Moreno, who was also devout. She helped him sell firewood.

After exchanging a few more family stories, Laura and I left the coffee shop and headed back to the university. On the way, we passed by an old smoke shop. "That looks like our store in Brisbane," she said. "Let's go in." The place was small, dimly lit, and crowded. The shelves were jammed with cigar boxes of different sizes and shapes. Some had broken covers and faded labels. In the back corner of the room sat a pinball machine. Its blinking lights reflecting off the dark ceiling were the only cheerful spot in the store.

"Do you want to play a game?" she said, pulling the lever and quickly releasing it. I reached into my pants pocket, pulled out a quarter, and put it into the slot machine. "It's only a nickel a game," she said.

"Good, we'll play five games." She insisted I go first. Within seconds, I lost the first game. Sheepishly, I stepped aside, giving her room to take over. She released the first ball with such force that it shot forward, ringing bells and turning on multicolored lights. She swayed her shoulders and moved her arms and hands, trying to guide the ball to the top of the board. In perfect succession, five bells went off and a number 10 in red flashed on the scoreboard.

"I've won ten games!"

"You're a pro." We continued playing, she winning and I losing. Neither of us thought of time or homework. We left the shop determined to return to challenge the pinball machine, which we did whenever we went out together. It was perfect. Our friendship grew and our entertainment cost us only a nickel.

An American Citizen

Telling Laura my secret about being born in Mexico and not in Colton, California, finally lifted a heavy burden of guilt I had carried with me since childhood. Now I felt I had to confess it to Father John Shanks too. As my spiritual advisor, he met with me periodically to discuss my progress as a member of Sodality. At one of our meetings, I told him my story.

"I'm glad you told me. One should always tell the truth." His serious tone made me feel uncomfortable. "However, I understand why it has been difficult for you to be honest about where you were born, but you're here legally now, so try to get over it." He grinned slightly and lit up a cigarette.

"But I've lied about it in all my school records, in my application for admission to Santa Clara, and in my applications for financial aid from Santa Clara and the federal government."

He stared wide-eyed at me for a few seconds, taking a deep puff. "There is no problem with Santa Clara, but I am not sure about the federal loan." My heart fell to my stomach. Could I lose my scholarship?

"You would have heard from the federal government by now if it were a problem," he said, noticing my anxiety. "Why don't you become an American citizen? It would simplify matters."

Even though I was born in Mexico and was proud of being Mexican, I felt I was an American too. I had lived most of my life in the United States. It had become part of me. "I'd like to, but I don't know how."

"Well, that's a task for both of us. We'll start by getting you an application form."

A week later, Father Shanks handed me the petition for naturalization form and asked me to work on it. I read through the long document and was happy to find out that I qualified to apply for citizenship because I was an adult and had been living in the United States legally for eight years; the minimum was five. The application called for two witnesses from each of the places in which I had lived during the past five years. They had to be U.S. citizens and willing to give testimony in court, under oath, on my behalf. I asked Darlene Jiménez, Roberto's wife, and Eva Martínez, a family friend, from Santa Maria. Both agreed. Father Shanks asked Brian Servatius and Ron Whitcanack, two students at Santa Clara, to be my witnesses. They knew me well. Brian was a senior, president of Sodality, and a prefect in McLaughlin Hall. Ron was a classmate of mine and co-director of the Sodality Tutoring Cell. I completed the application form, writing down "Tlaquepaque, Mexico" for my place of birth. Writing down the truth felt strange but liberating.

A few days later, after I had mailed the petition, I received a letter from the United States Department of Justice in San Francisco informing me that I had to go to their headquarters to take an examination. I had to prove that I could speak, read, and write English. On Friday, February 12, I borrowed Tom Maulhardt's Volvo and drove to the Immigration and Naturalization building at 630 Sansome Street in San Francisco to take the test. I felt nervous but confident that I would pass.

James Welsh, the court clerk, greeted me and informed me that he would be administering the exam. He was an elderly, short, and balding gray-haired man who wore a rumpled dark gray suit and bow tie. His cramped office had a glass window that looked onto a larger office. I sat at a small worktable, to the right of his paper-cluttered desk. Adjusting his wire-rimmed glasses, he asked me questions on U.S. history and the Constitution: "In what year did the United States declare its independence? What are the three branches of government, and what is their function? How many articles of amendments to the Constitution are there? What is the Thirteenth Amendment?" I answered them all correctly. He then gave me a form with two sets of yes-or-no questions. I read through the first set and checked no to each question: "Are you now, or have you ever, in the United States or in any other place, been a member of, or in any other way connected or associated with, the Communist Party? Do you now or have you ever advocated, taught, believed in, or knowingly supported or furthered the interests of Communism? Have you borne any hereditary title or have you been of any order of nobility in any foreign state? Do you owe any federal taxes? Have you ever been a patient in a mental institution, or have you ever been treated for a mental illness?" The image of my father's gaunt face flashed in my mind as I read this last question.

I began the second set, checking yes to each question with confidence: "Do you believe in the U.S. Constitution and form of government of the United States? Are you willing to take the full oath of allegiance to the United States? If male, did you ever register under United States Selective Service laws or draft laws?"

However, when I got to the last two questions, my self-confidence quickly disappeared. I could hear my heart pounding as I reread them: "Are deportation proceedings pending against you, or have you ever been deported or ordered deported, or have you ever applied for suspension of deportation or for preexamination? Have you ever represented yourself to be a United States citizen?" I did not want to answer them but had no choice. My hand trembled as I checked yes and gave a brief explanation for each.

After I completed the questionnaire, the clerk dictated

a sentence to me: "I like the American way of life." I wrote it down, hoping that he would not ask me to explain "the American way of life." He picked up the questionnaire, glanced at it, and frowned. "Excuse me," he said. "I'll be right back." Through the window, I could see him in the larger office talking to a man who was dressed in a suit and tie. I guessed he was the supervisor. My mouth was dry and I had a tight feeling in my chest. *They are going to turn me down,* I thought. When the clerk returned, I said a quick silent prayer. "Your petition is complete," he said, closing the door behind him and placing the questionnaire on his desk. "All the depositions are in and you have passed the exam. Congratulations!"

I stood up and shook his hand. I was elated.

"You can expect to hear from us in about a month."

As I was about to leave, I glanced down at the question-naire and spotted a scribbled note in the margin, next to the last two questions, but I could not make out what it said. He caught my eye and grinned.

On April 2, I received a second letter from the United States Department of Justice. I nervously opened it and sat down at my desk to read. "You are hereby notified to appear for a hearing on your petition for naturalization before a judge of the naturalization court on Tuesday, April 13, at Ceremonial Court, Room 415, U.S. Courthouse, 450 Golden Gate Avenue, San Francisco, California. Please report promptly at 8:15 AM. Certificates of naturalization will be mailed by the Clerk of Court within five (5) days after your admission to citizenship."

I anxiously showed the letter to Father Shanks. He assured me that I had been approved for citizenship, that the hearing was simply ceremonial.

On the day of the hearing, I got up at dawn and hurried to the Santa Clara train station, which was a few blocks from the university. I bought a roundtrip ticket to San Francisco and took a window seat. As the train pulled out of the station, I thought about the long train trip my family and I had made when I was four years old.

Our journey from Guadalajara to Mexicali on a second-class train, Ferrocarriles Naciones de Mexico, took two days and nights. I was excited and impatient to get to California because my father repeatedly told us that life would be better there. When we arrived at the United States–Mexico border, Roberto, my parents, and I waited until night to cross the barbed-wire fence, which separated the two countries. We walked several miles along the wire wall, away from the entry point, until we spotted a small hole underneath the fence. My father got on his knees and dug a larger opening with his hands. We all slithered through like snakes and entered California.

The train to San Francisco jerked and grinded its brakes as it made the first stop. I looked out the window. The sun was beginning to rise.

About an hour later, the train arrived in San Francisco. I

took a city bus to McAllister Street and walked up to the Ceremonial Court Room in the United States Courthouse. The spacious room had a high ceiling and stained-glass windows. It quickly filled up with men and women who had also petitioned for citizenship. Some wore suits and ties, a few dressed in full-length white robes and colorful turbans, others wore casual clothes. I took a seat toward the front and overheard different languages being spoken. The court clerk came in and asked us to stand for the presiding judge. After making a few welcoming remarks, the judge administered the Oath of American Citizenship, and at the end of the ceremony we recited The Pledge of Allegiance, which I knew so well.

I pledge allegiance to the Flag of the United States of America and to the Republic for which it stands, one nation under God, indivisible, with liberty and justice for all.

Our voices filled the Ceremonial Court Room like a prayer. We all had emigrated to the United States from various countries and were now American citizens. We were all different yet the same.

Memories of a Barrack

A couple of days before going home for the summer at the end of the spring quarter of my junior year, I received a message that my brother had called and to call him right away, collect. I figured Roberto was calling me about the letter I sent him. "It has been the best year in college so far," I had written. "I am now an American citizen and got straight-As in my classes. Please tell the rest of our family." When I returned his call from the pay phone booth on the first floor of Walsh, Roberto accepted the call and told me how proud he was of my grades and citizenship. But I could tell by the sad tone of his voice that something was wrong.

"What's the matter? You sound down." I pressed my back against the glass door to secure it shut. "Is Papá all right?"

"Yes, Panchito. He's fine." His voice cracked. "The house in Bonetti Ranch burned down. No one got hurt, thank God, but almost everything is gone."

I did not want to believe it. I lightly hit my head several times against the black pay phone casing. "How, when?" I asked.

"It happened a few of weeks ago. We—"

"Why didn't you tell me then?"

"We didn't want you to worry during finals."

I should have guessed. "I'm sorry. I'm not angry at you, Toto."

"I know, I understand."

He went on to tell me how the fire began. The electrical wiring in our barrack was faulty, which explained why the fuses blew out frequently. The wires heated up and caused a short circuit, which started the fire. Anticipating my next question, he added, "Mamá, Trampita, Torito, Rorra, and Rubén stayed with us for a few days until we found a rental house in town for them to stay. It's a bit too small for everyone, so you'll be staying with us during the summer."

After our conversation, I went to the Mission Church, knelt down, and prayed before the painting of St. Francis at the Cross. I felt depressed. This wasn't the first time our family had suffered from a fire.

Many years before, in September, the week I was to begin the seventh grade, we moved as usual to the San Joaquin Valley to harvest grapes after spending the summer picking strawberries in Santa Maria for Ito, the Japanese sharecropper. We made our new home in an old two-story yellow house located about fifteen miles outside of Orosi, a small town near Fresno. It was the first house we had ever lived in. Mr. Patrini, the owner for whom we picked grapes, told us we could not use the second level because the floors were unstable. The first floor had two rooms and a kitchen with a kerosene stove, which sat on a small table underneath a window that had plastic curtains. We bought kerosene for the stove from a gas station in town, using a five-gallon can. One day, the gas station attendant mistakenly filled the can with gasoline, which we poured into the kerosene stove. When my mother lit the range, it burst into flames, setting the wooden house on fire. Pieces of melted plastic fell to the floor, giving off dark smoke that smelled like burned rubber. Roberto picked up a dishpan full of soapy water and hurled it over the stove. It was like adding gasoline to the fire. The flames quickly spread on the floor, and by the time the firefighters came, the house had burned to the ground.

My mother had consoled me after I had lost my prized notepad in that fire. I used the small notepad to jot down words I needed to learn for school and memorized them while I worked in the fields so that I would not be too far behind when I started classes for the first time every year in November. She had reminded me to be thankful to God that none of us in the family was injured and pointed out that all was not lost because I had learned everything I had written in my notepad by heart.

When I returned to my dorm, I told Father Shanks about our house burning down and asked him to pray for my family.

A few days later, when I left for home, he gave me a sympathy note and one hundred dollars from Father

William Perkins, vice president of Student Services. The note read: "You and your family are in my prayers."

Shortly after I arrived at my brother's house, he and I drove to see the rest of my family in our new rental home. It was a two-bedroom tract house built in the late 1940s on the west side of the city. When I walked in the door, they were as happy to see me as I was to see them. My mother looked tired but calm. She was wearing lipstick, which I had never seen her use before. "I am glad to see you." She gave me a hug.

"I am sorry the house burned down." I wasn't sure what else to say.

"Así es la vida, mijo," she said. Such is life, son. *"Pero no hay mal que por bien no venga."* But every dark cloud has a silver lining. She told me how it was more comfortable living there than in Bonetti Ranch. The house had a toilet and shower and the water was drinkable. "And the rent is only a little bit higher," she added.

"I'm glad, Mamá." I handed her the envelope that Father Perkins had given me. "It's a gift from the Jesuits."

She opened it. *"Gracias a Dios!"* she exclaimed. Her eyes welled up. "This will help us get a few more things we need. And with your summer earnings, we'll be okay."

Rubén and Rorra excitedly told me that they now could sleep longer in the mornings because they could walk to school instead of taking a bus. Torito talked about his freshman year in high school. "I wanted to take shop classes," he said, "but Mr. Penney, my counselor, told me I had to take college prep courses. 'You have to go to college,' he told me."

"Good," I said.

"Torito has a girlfriend," Rorra said.

My brother blushed and rolled his eyes.

"Show Panchito her picture," Rubén said. He and Rorra glanced at each other and giggled.

"Go on, *mijo*," my mother said. "Show it to him. Marcy is a very nice and beautiful girl."

Torito went to his room and brought back a small color photo of his girlfriend and handed it to me. She had a round face, brown skin, short jet black hair, and almond-shaped eyes.

"She's beautiful," I said, passing it back to him.

"Marcy is really smart," Roberto said. "She helps Torito with his homework."

I was surprised that Trampita did not tease Torito about Marcy's helping him with his schoolwork. He listened to our conversation but remained silent.

"How are things going?" I asked after a few minutes, directing my attention to him.

"Okay," he said, glancing at a smoke-damaged crucifix hanging on the wall that was salvaged from the fire.

"Just okay?"

"I like it here, but I miss Bonetti Ranch."

"Why?" Roberto asked.

"It's hard to explain. I've written a poem about it," he added.

"Read it to us," I said.

"No, I'll give it to you. You can read it later."

As Roberto and I were leaving, Trampita gave me his poem in a large manila envelope. That evening, before going to bed, I read it. The title was *"Mi Casa* No Longer Shames Me."

> Mouth is wet
> With seasons met
> Recalling . . .
> Living in barracks
> Of war's pretense
> Trophies of ruins,
> Old and worn
> To house the scorned
> For being born
> Poor.

. . . .

> After school we were the first
> Off the bus.
> My friends asked where I lived.
> Ashamed I would say:
> "That one." Then I would get off
> At a house that was
> Not my own;
> White like snow,

Grass like jade,
And walked home ashamed and confused;
Feeling used.

. . . .

I recall that house
Ashamed I was
Of where I lived.
I never told my mamá
For I could not understand
This feeling I knew
Was not right
That I should feel ashamed
Of the warmth she gave,
Of the home she made.

. . . .

We finally moved to town.
It was after that night
That I came home
And found our house
Burning down.
The sky was red
With flames it spat,
Flashing lights, fire trucks,

Faces made of stone.
All hope gone,
Destroyed by the flames
Of mighty feat.
Eyes watering, flooding our sighs
Already so familiar with pain,
Wondering why our tears did not
Extinguish those flames.
My soul died again and again.

I've visited that place again
Many times.
Still, families live there.
New faces, familiar sounds,
Familiar souls.

Yes! I recall that house.
The *casa* that no longer
Shames me.

The next morning I drove to Bonetti Ranch and visited
the place where our barrack once stood. Only bits of broken glass and scorched metal and twisted wire and ashes
remained. The large pepper tree that had provided shade
was also damaged. Its charred branches hung down,
mourning the loss of a good friend. I remained there for a
long time remembering our old barrack, which provided us

with shelter for so many years, protecting us from cold, wind, and rain, and from an outside world that at times was confusing and unfriendly.

In Solidarity

At the beginning of the third quarter of my senior year, I made a decision with which my mother strongly disagreed and which affected my midterm grade in my ethics class: I decided to support César Chávez's efforts to unionize farm workers. "We'll lose our jobs; we'll get fired if we go on strike, *mijo*," my mother told me. "Who's going to feed our family while we're out of work?" I explained to her that by workers' going on strike and joining the National Farm Worker's Association growers would be forced to provide us and other farm workers with unemployment insurance and better working conditions and guarantee a minimum wage. "*Ay, mijo, piénsalo bien*," she said. Think about it carefully. "Growers have all the power. Poor farm workers like us don't have a chance against them." I stopped arguing with her out of respect. Besides, I understood her fears.

I became more convinced I had made the right decision after attending a forum on the issue of farm workers that took place at noon on Monday, April 4, in front of the student union. Father Tenant Wright, a young and energetic

Jesuit priest who organized the event, stood in the middle of a small group of students and asked, "Is it necessary to form a union to represent farm labor?" He looked around and shouted the same question, beckoning students who were passing by to join the growing crowd. As the gathering grew, I spotted Laura several feet away. I elbowed my way through and stood next to her. I was glad she was there.

Father Wright explained the purpose of the forum. He said that the Delano grape strike began seven months before when farm workers in Delano walked off the farms of table grape growers, demanding wages on a level with the federal minimum wage. The strike was being led by César Chávez and Dolores Huerta of the National Farm Workers Association. They were asking farm workers to join their labor union. "Again, is this necessary?" Father Wright asked. "To help us answer this question, I have invited two people to speak to this issue."

Father Wright introduced Frank Bergon, the son of a grower, who presented the growers' position, and Les Grube, an egg distributor and longtime activist in Catholic welfare programs, who defended the NFWA's viewpoint. Bergon argued that the farm laborers were already well paid and that the number of strikers was small.

"How can he say that?" I whispered, rolling my eyes and shaking my head. Farm laborers were paid eighty-five cents an hour and sometimes less.

"Why don't you say something?" Laura whispered.

I felt my heart pounding and a fire in my stomach, but I was still shy about speaking out in groups. I knew I was disappointing Laura and wished I had not been with her at that moment. She excused herself and left for class.

After the debate I picked up a flyer from the NFWA representative and hurried back to my room to prepare for my ethics class that afternoon. I completed the reading assignment in our textbook *Right and Reason* and then read the flyer. It was an open invitation from César Chávez to join him on a march to Sacramento.

On March 17, 1966, the National Farm Workers Association will begin a 300-mile "Peregrinación" from Delano to Sacramento. It is a march of farm workers. It will begin in Delano and will involve workers from all parts of the state. . . .It will be a pilgrimage by members of all races and religions. In order to be successful, we will need the help of our friends around the state and nation. We ask you to . . . join us for a day on the march and especially for the last day in Sacramento. Although this is primarily a march of farm workers, it is important that all who have a concern for social justice and human dignity demonstrate their unity with us.

I set the flyer down on my desk and paced the floor, thinking about whether or not I should join the march. I had learned in Sodality and my religion and philosophy classes that it was a moral obligation to fight for social justice. Father Shanks had told us that leaders must have a strong sense of personal responsibility and give something of themselves to make a difference in society. In my mind joining the march was the right thing to do, but I also felt this in my heart as I thought of my family and other migrant laborers working in the fields from dawn to dusk, seven days a week, living in army tents and suffering hunger during cold winter months when there was no work. I remembered my mother weeping and praying for Torito, who was dying, and we had no money to take him to the doctor. I remembered my father agonizing from constant back pain and reaching out to me when I found him alone in the storage shed. I remembered Gabriel, a *bracero*, being fired because he refused to tie a rope around his waist and pull a plow like an ox. I heard his words in my head: *"Díaz me puede correr. Pero no puede forzarme a hacer lo que no es justo. El no puede quitarme la dignidad. Eso no lo puede hacer."* Díaz can fire me. But he can't force me to do what isn't right. He can't take away my dignity. That he can't do.

A wave of sadness and anger came over me. I had to join the pilgrimage to Sacramento.

At the end of my ethics class, I told Father Charles McQuillan, the instructor, that I would be missing class on Thursday because I had decided to join the march to Sacramento. He reminded me that we had an exam on that day. "I am assuming you thought about this carefully and know the consequences," he said, adjusting his Roman collar.

"Yes. But I was hoping you would let me make up the test."

"You know I don't give makeups."

"Yes, I know, but . . . "

"So, is sacrificing your grade to go on the march worth it?" he asked, looking me in the eye.

I didn't hesitate. "It is."

"Then go ahead. Sometimes we have to make sacrifices for what we believe in." He smiled and shook my hand.

I thanked him and headed to see Jerry McGrath, the dean of students, who had hired me again that year to be a prefect. I needed his approval to leave campus. I was glad that he was already aware of the march and supported it. He authorized my request. I then asked Tim Taormina, my roommate with whom I shared prefect responsibilities, if he would cover for me. Tim agreed to take over my duties in exchange for my standing in for him the following two weekends.

Three days before Easter, on Holy Thursday morning, April 7, at five a.m., Jerry McGrath drove four other students and me in an eight-passenger van for an hour and a half until we spotted the tail end of the pilgrimage. It was a long, thin, serpentine line inching its way along the flat Central Valley on Highway 99, near the city of Lodi. He dropped us off and we joined the peaceful journey to Sacramento. I hurried toward the front of the procession, leaving my schoolmates behind.

Several feet in front of me walked César Chávez. He was flanked by farm workers carrying the American flag, the Mexican flag, the flag from the Philippines, and a large banner of the Virgen de Guadalupe. Excited to see him, I tried to bypass other marchers to get closer, but one of the monitors stopped me and asked me to fall back in line. I ended up behind a young man who wore shorts, a white T-shirt, a Giants cap, and a red armband with an Aztec black eagle. I looked behind me and saw an older man who reminded me of my father. His face and hands were weather-beaten. He wore khaki pants, a long-sleeve shirt, and a sweat-stained cap. In each hand he carried a *huelga*, a flag. When I smiled at him, he stretched out his arm to hand me one of his strike flags.

The blazing sun hung above the pale blue sky. I could feel the blistering asphalt on the bottoms of my tired feet as we continued walking by hundreds of acres of green fields that stretched for miles on either side of Highway 99. My family had traveled this same road every year, for nine years, looking for work during the grape and cotton seasons. We had passed through Tulare, Visalia, Selma, Fowler, Parlier, and Fresno. At a distance, I spotted a yellow crop-duster sweeping over the fields, leaving a trail of gray clouds behind. It reminded me of picking strawberries and having to crouch down as crop-dusters flew above our heads and sprayed the fields with chemicals that caused our eyes to burn and water for days. Today I felt anger and pity

when I saw farm workers bent over thinning sugar beets
with the same type of short-handle hoes that Roberto and
I used when we thinned lettuce in Santa Maria. I could feel
their back pain from stooping all day. The farm workers
slowly straightened up and watched us. "*Vénganse con noso-
tors,*" one of the organizers yelled out, trying to persuade
them to join the march. The farm workers waved and continued working. *They must be afraid, like my mother, to lose
their jobs,* I thought.

As passersby honked their car horns and waved, I smiled
and raised my flag. One pickup driver flipped us off and
yelled out the window, "Go back to Mexico!"

What an idiot, I thought, fuming inside. Along the way,
local supporters joined us for a while; others offered us rice
and bean tacos and water for lunch.

That night we gathered outside of Galt, a small town
where the organizers had planned a program for us. They
passed out flyers to residents, asking them to boycott table
grapes and all Schenley products until Schenley recognized
the National Farm Workers Association. We were given
copies of "El Plan de Delano," which described the purpose for the march to Sacramento. We chanted "*Sí se
puede.*" Yes we can. We sang songs like "De Colores." Luis
Valdez, a stocky and vigorous young man with jet black hair
and a Zapata-style mustache, jumped onto a makeshift
wooden platform and began reading "El Plan de Delano"
in a deep and powerful voicc.

This is the beginning of a social movement in fact and not in pronouncements. We seek our basic, God-given rights as human beings. Because we have suffered—and are not afraid to suffer—in order to survive, we are ready to give up everything, even our lives, in our fight for social justice. We shall do it without violence because that is our destiny . . .

We seek, and have, the support of the Church in what we do. At the head of the Pilgrimage we carry LA VIRGEN DE LA GUADALUPE because she is ours, all ours, Patroness of the Mexican people. We also carry the Sacred Cross and the Star of David because we are not sectarians, and because we ask the help and prayers of all religions. All men are brothers, sons of the same God . . .

Our men, women, and children have suffered not only the basic brutality of stoop labor, and the most obvious injustices of the system; they have also suffered the desperation of knowing that the system caters to the greed of callous men and not to our needs. Now we will suffer for the purpose of ending the poverty, the misery, and the injustice, with the hope that our children will not be exploited as we have been . . .

We shall unite. We have learned the meaning of UNITY. We know why these United States are just that—united. The strength of the poor is also in union. We know that the poverty of the Mexican or Filipino worker in California is the same as that of all farm workers across the country, the Negroes and poor whites, the Puerto Ricans, Japanese, and Arabians; in short, all of the races that comprise the oppressed minorities of the United States. The majority of the people on our Pilgrimage are of Mexican descent, but the triumph of our race depends on a national association of all farm workers . . .

We shall strike . . . We want to be equal with all the working men in the nation; we want a just wage, better working conditions, a decent future for our children. To those who oppose us . . . we say that we are going to continue fighting until we die, or we win. WE SHALL OVERCOME.

The time has come for the liberation of the poor farm worker.

History is on our side.
MAY THE STRIKE GO ON!
¡VIVA LA CAUSA!
¡VIVA LA HUELGA!

"*Viva la causa! Viva la huelga!*" we all shouted. Hurray for the cause. Hurray for the strike. I felt a wave of energy I had never experienced before. When César Chávez took the stage, we quieted down. He thanked us for our support and said, "If you are outraged at conditions, then you cannot possibly be free or happy until you devote all your time to changing them and do nothing but that. Fighting for social justice, it seems to me, is one of the profoundest ways in which men can say yes to human dignity, and that really means sacrifice. The best source of power, the best source of hope, is straight from you, the people. The boycott is not just grapes and lettuce. The boycott is essentially people, essentially people's concern for people." His words about sacrificing and caring for others echoed the ideas I had learned in Sodality and in my ethics class. They touched me and gave me courage.

That evening we were hosted by local families whose homes were like many of the places my family had lived in: small farm workers' cabins with no electricity or running water. Some marchers slept outside on the grass, others underneath trees.

On Easter Sunday thousands of us entered Sacramento. We swarmed the capitol steps, where César Chávez announced that Schenley had agreed to recognize the union. We all clapped and shouted with joy "*Sí se puede!*" for several minutes. After thanking the unions, the church, and all the students and civil rights workers who had helped win this one victory, César Chávez told us: "*Es bueno recordar que debe haber valor, pero también que, en la victoria, debe haber humildad.*" It is well to remember there must be courage, but also, that in victory there must be humility.

As he continued speaking, I looked at the banner of the Virgen de Guadalupe and felt deeply the suffering and pain of migrant workers. *What can and should I do in my life to help them?* I asked myself. I did not have the answer yet.

Providence

During my junior year I had begun taking required education courses to become a teacher. Father Louis Bannan, a Jesuit priest, from whom I took Psychology of Education, encouraged me to pursue a high school teaching career. He was gentle and kind like Mr. Lema, my sixth grade teacher. He taught by continually asking questions, which engaged us in heated but respectful discussions. My plans to become a high school teacher, however, were changed a few months before graduation.

The fall quarter of my senior year, I received a letter in the campus mail from Professor Bernard Kronick, chairman of the Political Science Department and director of fellowships, informing me that I had been nominated by the university for a Woodrow Wilson Fellowship. He asked that I come by his office to pick up the application form. After my afternoon class, I went to see him.

"Thank you for coming. Please have a seat," he said in a low and reserved voice. He was a short, stocky man with glasses and was bald over the front and top of his head. He loosened his tie and took off his tight-fitting sport coat and draped it over the back of his chair. "Congratulations, Frank," he said, leaning forward and handing me a large envelope. "This is the application form you need to fill out."

"Thank you." I took the envelope and placed it on my lap.

"The Woodrow Wilson Fellowship program is designed to encourage college graduates to consider college teaching as a career."

"But I am planning to teach high school."

"Have you thought of teaching at the college level?"

"No." I shook my head.

"Well, you shouldn't rule it out. As I said, these national fellowships are to encourage bright students, like you, to pursue college teaching. Think about it."

"I will," I responded halfheartedly, glancing down at the thick envelope.

"It's already an honor to be nominated, so don't be too disappointed if you're not awarded one. These fellowships are very competitive."

I thanked him and went back to my room, sat at my desk, and opened the envelope. I read through the application, thinking, *I am not smart enough to teach in college.* That evening, after closing the language lab, I told Laura about being nominated for the fellowship.

"That's wonderful. Congratulations!"

When I told her that I wasn't sure I should apply, that the

application was really long and I didn't have time to fill it out, she said, "You've got to be kidding!"

I remained silent for a few seconds as she patiently waited for a response. I glanced at her and then looked down and said, "I don't think I have a chance."

"Of course you do," she said, smiling. "Why would the university nominate you if you didn't?" Suddenly I felt more weight on my shoulders. "If you don't apply, you won't get the fellowship," she added.

I worked on the application every day for several days. I wrote a personal statement describing my childhood experiences and explaining why I wanted to be a teacher. I asked Father Shanks, Dr. Vari, and Father O'Neill for letters of recommendation. (Unfortunately, Dr. Hardman de Bautista had left the university, so I could not ask her for one.) A few weeks later, after I had mailed the application, I received a letter from the Woodrow Wilson Foundation informing me that I was a regional finalist.

I felt happy but, again, worried. The possibility of going to graduate school for a doctorate scared me. When I found out that I had an interview the following week at Stanford University where the regional finalists were being screened, I felt even more tense. I rushed to see Father O'Neill to tell him about it.

"Good for you," he said, in his soft, raspy voice. He stood up and shook my hand. "Good for you," he repeated. He sat down slowly and placed his trembling hands on his lap.

"I am worried about the interview. I don't think I'll do well."

"Of course you will. You have to be confident. Remember, God is on your side. When is the interview?"

"Next week, Wednesday at two o'clock."

"You should dress nicely. Wear the suit Mrs. Hancock gave you."

"It's too big," I said. Even though it had been two years, I still couldn't get her husband's pinstriped suit to fit.

"Oh . . . it doesn't matter," he said thoughtfully. "Just be sure to wear a tie." He got up slowly, moved behind his desk chair, and braced himself on the back of it with both hands. "Can you do me a favor and accompany me to Macy's at Valley Fair? I need to buy some socks. It won't take long."

"Sure. I'd be happy to." I wondered why he invited me, but I thought it would be disrespectful to say no. As we headed to the Jesuit parking lot in the back of Varsi, I noticed he leaned slightly forward and his shoulders drooped a bit more than they had the year before. We drove to the large shopping center, which was about three miles from campus, and parked the white two-door sedan near Macy's. I followed him to the men's department, where he picked up three pairs of black socks. He then made his way to the suit section and began examining various styles and colors. "What size suit do you wear?" he asked.

"I'm not sure."

"Here, try this one on." He took a blue suit jacket off the

rack. "It's a forty regular."

"Oh, I can't afford to buy a suit."

"It doesn't cost anything to try it on. Try it." He grabbed on to the side of the rack as I slipped it on.

"It's too long." I looked at the price tag and frowned.

He caught my eye, smiled, and shook his head.

"You must wear a thirty-eight short." He rifled through the row of suits with his right hand while holding on to the top of the rack with his left one. "Here's one! It's light green. Do you like it?"

At this point I suspected that he was going to offer to buy it for me.

"Yes," I said, trying on the jacket. It fit perfectly. I grabbed the hanger and hung the jacket back with the trousers. I was about to place the suit back on the rack when Father O'Neill snatched it from me.

"You're wearing this to your interview," he said firmly. "I'm buying it for you."

I was speechless, even though I had guessed he wanted to buy it. My eyes welled up as I looked up at him. Giving me time to compose myself, he added, "Actually, I am not exactly buying it. The Jesuit community is."

After what seemed an eternity, I finally said, "Thank you, Father. I'm sorry I don't have the words to tell you how much I appreciate this."

"You're welcome. Someday, you'll do the same for someone else."

I had the suit pants tailored to fit, and two days later, Father O'Neill and I picked them up at Macy's. He also bought me a white shirt and tie to match the suit. When we returned to his office, he gave me an apple and an orange and a set of plain square-shaped, gold-colored cufflinks.

"I want you to have these," he said, grinning. "I've had them for years. I have another pair."

I thanked him several times. As I was about to leave, he added, "Don't forget—keep your head up. You'll do just fine in your interview. Trust in God."

The day of the interview, I was as nervous as I had been the first day of classes my freshman year. I felt sick to my stomach. I attended early-morning Mass at the Mission Church and had a slice of toast with strawberry jam and a cup of tea for breakfast. After my two morning classes, I went back to my room, put on my new suit, had a light lunch in Benson, and drove to Stanford University in Ernie DeGasparis's Volkswagen, which I had borrowed from him the night before. As I headed north on Highway 101, I regretted having to miss my afternoon class on contemporary Latin American literature. This was the third time I had missed a class in college.

The closer I got to Stanford, the more anxious I became. I took the Embarcadero Road exit, which turned into Galvez Street. The entrance to the campus was lined with palm trees, just like the entrance to the University of Santa Clara. I parked the car near a cluster of eucalyptus trees, which smelled like sweet gum. Their distinct odor reminded me of the time my family and I first arrived in Santa Maria from Mexico when I was four years old. We had only seven dollars and no place to stay, so we spent the night on a bed of leaves underneath eucalyptus trees. I closed my eyes for a few seconds. *This feels like a dream,* I thought to myself.

I climbed out of the car and followed the directions to the quad, which had sandstone arches all around. I entered the main door to the History Corner and spotted a small sign that read WOODROW WILSON INTERVIEWS, RM. 105. I took a deep breath, wiped my clammy hands on the sides of my coat, straightened my clip-on tie, and knocked on the door.

A tall, thin man wearing a navy blue suit came out, greeted me, and introduced himself as Dr. Otis Pease. I remembered his name because it registered in my mind as Dr. *Chícharos,* the Spanish word for peas; however, I was so nervous that I did not learn the names of the other two men, who were also wearing suits and were very friendly. I sat at a rectangular wooden table facing them with my feet wrapped around the legs of the chair to stop my legs from shaking. Each committee member had a file folder, which I assumed contained my application and letters of recommendation. Dr. Pease, the chairman of the interview committee, began by commenting on my grades.

"Your academic record is impressive," he said, opening his folder and glancing at it. "You have a 3.8 GPA overall in your last two years and a 3.9 in your major. Now tell us about yourself and why you're interested in a teaching career."

While I spoke, the three men smiled periodically and glanced at each other. This made me feel more at ease. Once I finished my response, the other two interviewers engaged me in a discussion about Spanish literature and Latin American literature and history, for which I was thankful because I had taken several courses in the history of Mexico and South America from Dr. Matt Meier, one of my favorite professors. At the end of the interview, Dr. Pease informed me that his committee would be making a recommendation to the Woodrow Wilson National Committee, who in turn would be making a final decision.

A few days later, I received a letter from Hans Rosenhaupt, national director of the Woodrow Wilson National Fellowship Foundation. It read:

> *The Selection Committee which interviewed you has recommended you for an award and the National Selection Committee has accepted the recommendation. I am happy to offer you a Woodrow Wilson Fellowship for the academic year 1966–1967.*
>
> *Since only 1,400 Fellows were elected this year from over 13,000 carefully chosen nominees, this election demonstrates great confidence in your promise as a teacher and scholar. From funds supplied by the Ford Foundation, Woodrow Wilson Fellows receive a living stipend, free tuition and fees at a graduate school of their*

choice, and their graduate school receives an additional subvention.

While a Woodrow Wilson Fellow is not obliged to become a college teacher, he is expected to complete one year of graduate study and to give serious thought to a career in college teaching. . . .

The members of the National Selection Committee and the trustees join me in warm congratulations on the honor bestowed upon you.

I could not believe it. I read the letter twice to make sure it was addressed to me. That I would not have to work as a prefect for room and board or take out loans from the federal government was also impossible to believe. I said a prayer before the image of the Virgen de Guadalupe tacked above my desk and dashed out of my room to thank and share the good news with everyone at the university who was close to me—Father Shanks, Father O'Neill, Dr. Vari, Laura, Emily, and Smokey. I called Roberto and Darlene and told them. They were as thrilled as I was and promised to tell the rest of the family.

Once I calmed down that evening, a wave of fear came over me. What if I didn't have time to work while I was in graduate school to help my family? What if I failed graduate school? These thoughts kept me awake all night. The next morning, I felt exhausted and discouraged. I reread the letter and hurried to Walsh Hall to see Father Shanks.

"You need to have more self-confidence, Frank. There is no doubt in my mind that you'll succeed in graduate school. You wouldn't have been awarded the fellowship if you weren't capable of handling graduate work. Just think, with a doctorate you'll be able to teach at a university or be a consultant to our government on international relations. With regard to your family, don't worry. Graduate fellowships provide stipends for dependents." Learning that fellowships made funds available for dependents, and his confidence in me, eased my worries. I could use grant money to help support my family.

Two weeks before graduation I received a second letter from Hans Rosenhaupt encouraging me to attend Columbia University rather than Emory University, the two graduate schools to which I was advised to apply at the time I was nominated for the Woodrow Wilson Fellowship. He wrote: "Considering the academic advantages, also the possibility of continued support at Columbia, I would urge you to accept Columbia's offer. Let me know by collect telegram if you are willing to attend Columbia University."

After sending the telegram to the Woodrow Wilson Foundation informing them that I would be attending Columbia, I made a visit to the Mission Church and gave thanks for this unexpected blessing.

Commencement

"In a couple of days I'll be graduating from Santa Clara," I told myself as I finished taking my ethics final, the last exam of my college career. I turned in my blue book to Father McQullian and left the classroom feeling happy and relieved. On the way to my room in Dunne, I passed by the olive trees lining the Mission Gardens and looked at the lush green lawn and the tall date palms. The beds of red, pink, yellow, and white flowers planted around their base looked like colorful skirts. I sat on the front stairs of Varsi thinking about graduation and going to Columbia. I watched the little goldfish silently gliding in the pond. I glanced up and spotted a white cloud moving slowly across the light blue sky and followed it with my eyes as it changed shapes several times until it faded away.

Suddenly the thought of leaving Santa Clara made me feel sad. After graduation, I would no longer spend time with Laura, I would no longer visit Father O'Neill in his office and take walks with him, I would no longer see Emily and Smokey or go to after-game school dances or browse through the stacks in Orradre Library for enjoyment. My freshman year I had been eager to see time pass by quickly, especially when things were difficult at home. Now I wished for time to stop. I went back across the Mission Gardens and entered the Mission Church, where time often seemed to stand still. I knelt down and said a prayer before the painting of St. Francis at the Cross, the same one I had prayed to so many times before, and enjoyed the silence and the scent of incense and burning candles. I remained there for a long while and then returned to my room, feeling happy and sad at the same time.

On Friday night I called Roberto from the pay phone booth, which was two doors down the hall from my room, to give him the details about graduation. I shut the glass door tight and held my hand to my right ear to block out the noise coming from students who were celebrating the end of the school year.

"We're all excited, Panchito—tomorrow is the big day! We're driving up really early."

"Who's coming?

"Mom, Torito, Rubén, and Rorra are coming too, but not Trampita."

"Why not?"

"He couldn't get out of work."

I immediately felt disappointed and guilty. The noise in the hallway annoyed me. I opened the door halfway, poked my head out, and told students who were horsing around to be quiet. They gave me a dirty look.

"Whatever you say, Mr. Big Shot Prefect," I heard one of them say.

I won't be missing this, I thought. I slammed the door shut. "Sorry for the interruption," I said. "I feel really bad that Trampita is not coming."

"I know. Me too."

After a brief silence, Roberto added, "But he'll be there in spirit, just like Dad."

I felt my throat tighten. The last we had heard from Tía Chana about my father was that he was recovering from his depression but continued to suffer back problems. My mother and younger siblings had not lost hope for his return, but, like Trampita, Roberto and I had doubts. Our family talked about going to see him once we could afford the trip.

At the end of our conversation, we agreed to meet in front of the Mission Church right after commencement. That same evening I invited Emily and her mother and Laura to my graduation and made reservations for lunch at the Pine Cone Inn, a restaurant in Valley Fair that Father O'Neill had recommended.

Saturday morning, I climbed out of bed late after having spent half the night awake, thinking about graduation and wondering what my life would be like in New York. I took a shower and quickly got dressed in my black gown with long pointed sleeves and a white hood. I raced across campus, carrying my mortarboard cap in my right hand, and joined my classmates in line, which began in front of the Mission Church and snaked back to O'Connor Hall.

Looking like a lineup of penguins, my classmates and I anxiously waited for the commencement procession to begin. As soon as the U.S. Army band began playing "Pomp and Circumstance," we started moving slowly, passing the front of the Mission Church. We turned right at the end of it and continued under an arbor overflowing with purple wisteria flowers. We circled around the statue of the Sacred Heart, went through an archway in the adobe wall, and entered the Mission Gardens and began filling the rows of plastic chairs, facing a makeshift stage behind the Jesuit residence. The faculty and administrators marched at the end of the line and took their seats on stage. Wearing colorful gowns and caps of various shapes and sizes, they looked like a flock of peacocks. Thousands of spectators filled the Gardens all around, some sitting, others standing with small children on their shoulders.

After the Reverend Philip J. Oliger, chaplain of the university, gave the invocation, William P. Fay, the ambassador to Ireland, delivered the commencement address. I half listened to him, wondering whether or not my family had made the ceremony on time. I craned my neck, trying to spot them. My classmates and I became fidgety as an endless number of degree candidates from the School of Business and the School of Engineering were called individually on stage to receive their diplomas. Our restlessness vanished, however, when Father Thomas D. Terry, dean of the College of Arts and Sciences, was introduced. We all stood up and cheered as he presented our group to receive our diplomas. As it got closer to my name being called, I became increasingly excited and nervous. Finally I heard it. My heart raced ahead of me as I climbed the stairs to the stage. I felt as though I were in a dream, observing myself gliding in slow motion toward Father Patrick Donohoe, the president of the university, and reaching out for my certificate. Smiling and shaking my hand, he handed it to me. I clutched it against my chest with both hands and returned to my seat. *It happened too quickly,* I thought. I sighed, tuned out everything for a moment, and replayed the experience of graduation over and over in my head.

At the end of the ceremony, I made my way to the front of the Mission Church, where countless families and friends were hugging and congratulating graduates and taking pictures. I spotted my family, waved, and moved through the crowd to meet them. Roberto caught my eye and walked toward me, followed by the rest.

"We're proud of you, Panchito!" He gave me a strong, warm hug. I hugged him back, resting my chin on his broad shoulder.

"Congratulations—you did it!" Darlene exclaimed.

"We all did it," I responded. "I had a lot of help, especially from you and Toto."

"*¡Estoy muy orgullosa de ti, mijo!*" my mother said, tearing up and stroking my left cheek with her right hand. I'm so proud of you.

I embraced her. Torito, Rubén, and Rorra encircled us, locked hands, and hugged both of us. From the corner of my eye, I saw Emily and her mother and Laura standing on the side.

"Mamá, these are my best friends, Laura Facchini and Emily Bernabé and her mother."

"Pleased to meet you," my mother said, smiling and wiping her tears with a white embroidered handkerchief. Although I had not seen it for many years, I recognized it right away. I was surprised she still had it. My father had given it to her one Christmas. My family had moved to Corcoran that winter to pick cotton, after having picked grapes in Selma. It was a very difficult winter. It rained day after day, and we went weeks without work because we were not allowed to pick cotton when it was wet. Our family, like many other migrant families living in that labor camp, struggled to get by. A young man and his wife came to our cabin trying to sell their meager possessions to buy food. We were broke too, but my father wanted to help them. He bought the handkerchief, which the wife had embroidered, and surprised my mother with it on Christmas Day.

Remembering my father's goodness and loving gesture that Christmas made me miss him even more.

"Panchito has told me about all of you," my mother said. Then, directing her attention to Mrs. Bernabé, she said, "Thank you for taking care of Panchito and treating him like a son."

"He's a good boy . . . most of the time," Mrs. Bernabé said, winking at my mother.

"Panchito told me your cooking is just as good as mine," my mother said. Then with a big grin, she added, "You must be a great cook."

"You must be too," Mrs. Bernabé responded.

"Let me take a picture of the four of you," Darlene said, taking the camera from Roberto and snapping it: Laura and Emily standing to my right and Emily's mother to my left. After taking more pictures, we all headed to the Pine Cone Inn for lunch.

At the restaurant we sat at a long table near the entrance and ordered. Roberto, who was across from me, excused himself and returned with two gifts, a large one and a small one. He handed me the large one with a card. I read it silently:

> *Panchito, on our way to your graduation, I did a lot of thinking on the road. I was thinking of the way we used to live when we were little. What brought this to my mind was when I saw people working in the fields along the way near Gonzales. I also remembered the day you went off to college. I had mixed emotions. By this I mean I was happy for you but at the same time I didn't want you to go because I was going to miss you. I thought of your graduating from college and I feel so proud that my heart feels like bursting.*
>
> > *Love,*
> > *Toto*

"Thank you, Toto." I felt a lump in my throat. Darlene, who was sitting next to him, put her arm around him and tenderly kissed him on the cheek. I took a sip of water, cleared my throat, and tore the gift open. It was a small blue portable typewriter with a case.

"Darlene and I figured you'd need it at Columbia. Smokey won't be around to loan you his," he said, smiling and wiping his eyes.

"This is perfect. Thank you . . ." I placed it back in the box.

My mother began to choke up. "Columbia is so far, *mijo*. I wish you didn't have to go so far."

"Panchito needs to open another gift," Roberto said, noticing my uneasiness. "This one is from Mrs. Hancock." He handed me a card and a small box wrapped in blue paper. The card read: "The Captain and I are very proud of you. Congratulations and good luck at Columbia. Affectionately, Marian Hancock." Inside the box was a round, gold-colored wristwatch. I strapped it on my left hand and showed it off. Torito, who was sitting next to me, pulled my hand down to see it.

"It has no numbers; you won't be able to tell time."

"That's why I am going to Columbia. I need to learn my numbers, but time is on my side." Everyone booed politely at my bad joke.

After we finished eating, I raised my glass of water to make a toast: "I want to thank all of you for making a difference in my life. Thank you, Mamá, for your courage, faith, and love; Toto, for your sacrifices for our family and for being like a second father to me; Darlene, for your hospitality and love; Emily and Mrs. Bernabé, for giving me a home away from home; and Laura, for your friendship and wisdom and for accepting me for who I am."

"What about Torito, Rubén, and me?" Rorra protested.

"Thanks for being great brothers and a terrific sister . . . and for taking my pennies, Rorra." My sister made a bad face and crossed her arms, pretending to be upset. We looked at each other and laughed.

The waitress came by and handed me the check. Roberto tried to snatch it from me, but I quickly hid it behind my back. "Let me pay," he insisted. My brother was squeezed between my mother and Darlene, so he couldn't easily move away from the table. I rushed and paid the bill before he could get to the cashier. "I am your big brother and you have to obey me," he said half seriously.

"I know, but it's the least I can do to thank all of you for helping me."

"You've always been stubborn."

We left the restaurant in the middle of the afternoon and went back to the university. After we said goodbye to Emily and her mother, my family came up to my room in Dunne and rested while Laura and I went to visit Smokey and his wife, Mary, whom he had married during Christmas break of our senior year. They lived a few blocks away from campus, on Homestead Avenue. We stayed there briefly, and then I drove Laura to the Santa Clara train station to take the train back home to San Carlos. We sat in the car waiting for the train.

"I have a graduation gift for you," she said. She reached into her purse, pulled out a tiny box wrapped in yellow paper, and handed it to me.

"Thank you, but you didn't have to—"

"I know. I hope you like it."

I slowly unwrapped it, trying not to tear the paper, which was the same color as her dress. I carefully folded the wrapping, placed it in my shirt pocket, and opened the small black velvet box. "These are beautiful!" I took out a pair of oval-shaped gold-brushed cufflinks and a tie clip to match. "Thank you, thank you!" I reached over and gave her a kiss. We heard the train whistle.

"The train's coming," she said.

"I hate goodbyes," I said, feeling a pain in my chest.

"I do too." She had a sad smile on her face.

I got out of the car, went around it, and opened the door for her. "I'll write," I said. "Maybe I can borrow my brother's car and come up on a weekend during the summer and visit." My voice cracked.

"I'd like that very much."

She boarded the train, looked out the window, and waved goodbye. I waved back and followed the train with my eyes until it disappeared.

The days that summer seemed to go by more quickly than in previous summers even though the routine was the same: I worked for the Southern Counties Gas Company during the day, five days a week, painting meters and dispensing supplies from the warehouse, and in the evenings and on weekends for the Santa Maria Window Cleaners. Again, I lived with Roberto and Darlene and visited my mother, Trampita, Torito, Rubén, and Rorra only on Saturdays and Sundays after work. What differed, however, was that at the end of every day I went home excited, hoping to receive mail from friends I had made at Santa Clara, especially Laura, whom I visited once during that time. I could not see her more often because I had to work.

As time passed, I became more and more nervous and began to make preparations to leave home and move to New York. I bought a small used foot locker at the Salvation Army, packed it with my clothes and books, and shipped it by Greyhound bus to my new address: 817 John Jay Hall, Columbia University. I hated to move again. As a child, I had yearned for stability, for a place I could call my own. The sense of permanence that I had found living in Bonetti Ranch and at Santa Clara was now gone.

Saying goodbye to my family at the bus terminal on the day I left for Columbia was just as sad and difficult as the day I went to college my freshman year. This time, though, I was going far away. After hugging and kissing everyone, I boarded the bus. I took with me the card of the *Virgen de Guadalupe* that my father had given me on the first day of college, the portable typewriter, and the notebook in which I had jotted down recollections about my childhood experiences during college. I waved to my family from the window and cried silently, knowing that I would not see them again for an entire year. Travel was too expensive to come home for holidays.

In San José, I transferred to another bus that took me directly to the San Francisco International Airport. I went up to the airport counter to check in.

"Your name, please?" the attendant asked.

"Francisco Jiménez," I responded.

"Going to the Big Apple."

"Yes, I am going to graduate school to become a college teacher."

A Note from the Author

Reaching Out, like my previous works, *The Circuit: Stories from the Life of a Migrant Child* and *Breaking Through*, is autobiographical. In this book, I relate my experiences as a college student from an immigrant Mexican family of migrant workers. From the perspective of the young adult I was then, I describe the challenges I faced in my efforts to continue my education, such as coping with poverty, feeling torn between my responsibilities as a student and my sense of duty to my family, having self-doubt about being capable of succeeding academically, and trying to adjust to an environment that was different from the community in which I was raised.

In writing *Reaching Out,* I relied mostly on my memory but also on my powers of imagination and invention to fill in small details that I had forgotten with the passage of time. For example, when I could not remember some conversations word for word, I approximated or created dialogue and added description to capture the essence of my impressions and reactions to particular events and experiences.

Besides relying on the power of memory and inventiveness, I used other valuable resources to write my book. I interviewed family members, friends, classmates, and teachers. I looked through the few family photographs we had, as well as letters, yearbooks, the Santa Clara University student newspaper, my college research papers and essays and notes on my childhood memories, and official documents, including my school records and naturalization papers, which I obtained through the Freedom of Information Act.

I wrote *Reaching Out* in part to describe the experiences of many students who are the first in their immigrant families to attend college and to pay tribute to teachers who reach out and make a difference in the lives of their students by assisting them to be knowledgeable of self, educated in mind, compassionate in heart, and generous and responsive to social and civic obligations in an ever-changing world.

ABOVE: Francisco, Roberto, and Trampita in Tent City, Santa Maria, California.

ABOVE: Papá, Trampita, and Don Pancho, a family friend, at Bonetti Ranch. This is the only photo of his father from Francisco's childhood.

LEFT: Roberto and Francisco with their mother. This is the only photo of his mother from Francisco's childhood.

LEFT: The Mission Church, Santa Clara University.

LEFT: Smokey Murphy (on far right), Francisco's friend and college roommate.

BELOW: Victor B. Vari, professor of foreign languages, who mentored Francisco in college.

LEFT: Marian Hancock, who gave Francisco a Christmas job delivering presents.

BELOW LEFT TO RIGHT:
Father Bartholomew L. O'Neill,
S.J., and Father John Shanks,
S.J., Jesuit priests who mentored
Francisco in college.

ABOVE: Francisco's naturalization papers.

ABOVE: Francisco and Laura at Santa Clara University, getting ready to go on a picnic.

BELOW: Francisco's siblings and mother in a photo taken in 2000. TOP ROW, LEFT: Rubén, Torito, Roberto, Trampita; BOTTOM ROW, LEFT: Francisco, Rorra, Joaquina (Mamá).

ABOVE: Roberto and his wife, Darlene, newly married in Santa Maria.

ABOVE: Estefania Jiménez Hernandez, Francisco's paternal grandmother.

ABOVE: Graduation day with Emily Bernabé, Laura Facchini, Francisco, Juanita Bernabé.